THE
PROFESSOR
AND THE
PRESIDENT

THE
PROFESSOR
AND THE
PRESIDENT
DANIEL PATRICK MOYNIHAN
IN THE NIXON WHITE HOUSE

STEPHEN HESS

BROOKINGS INSTITUTION PRESS
Washington, D.C.

The Brookings Institution is a private nonprofit organization devoted to
research, education, and publication on important issues of domestic
and foreign policy. Its principal purpose is to bring the highest quality
independent research and analysis to bear on current and emerging policy
problems. Interpretations or conclusions in Brookings publications should
be understood to be solely those of the authors.

Library of Congress Cataloging-in-Publication data is available

ISBN 978-0-8157-2615-9 (cloth : alk. paper)
ISBN 978-0-8157-2616-6 (e-book)

9 8 7 6 5 4 3 2 1

Printed on acid-free paper

Typeset in Sabon and ITC Avant Garde

Composition by Cynthia Stock
Silver Spring, Maryland

To Liz

who held it all together

CONTENTS

THE CAST

Richard M. Nixon, *President of the United States*
Spiro T. Agnew, *Vice President of the United States*

The Cabinet

William Rogers, *Secretary of State*
David Kennedy, *Secretary of the Treasury*
Melvin Laird, *Secretary of Defense*
John Mitchell, *Attorney General*
Winton Blount, *Postmaster General*
Walter Hickel, *Secretary of the Interior*
Clifford Hardin, *Secretary of Agriculture*
Maurice Stans, *Secretary of Commerce*
George Shultz, *Secretary of Labor*
Robert Finch, *Secretary of Health, Education, and Welfare*
George Romney, *Secretary of Housing and Urban Development*
John Volpe, *Secretary of Transportation*

The White House

Arthur Burns, *Counselor to the President (cabinet rank)*
H. R. Haldeman, *Assistant to the President (chief of staff)*
John Ehrlichman, *Counsel to the President*
Henry Kissinger, *Assistant to the President for National Security Affairs*
Daniel Patrick Moynihan, *Assistant to the President for Urban Affairs*
Bryce Harlow, *Assistant to the President (congressional relations)*
Peter Flanigan, *Assistant to the President (personnel, business community)*
Leonard Garment, *Consultant to the President*
Charles (Bud) Wilkinson, *Consultant to the President (voluntary organizations)*
Herbert Klein, *Director of Communications for Executive Branch*
Stephen Hess, *Deputy Assistant to the President for Urban Affairs*
Ronald Ziegler, *Special Assistant to the President (press secretary)*
Martin Anderson, *Special Assistant to the President (aide to Arthur Burns)*
Dwight Chapin, *Special Assistant to the President (scheduling, appointments)*
Harry Flemming, *Special Assistant to the President (personnel)*
Pat Buchanan, *Special Assistant to the President (speeches)*
Ray Price, *Special Assistant to the President (speeches)*
William Safire, *Special Assistant to the President (speeches)*
Lee Huebner, *Staff Assistant to the President (speeches)*

Other Administration Officials

Donald Rumsfeld, *Director, Office of Economic Opportunity (cabinet rank)*

Paul McCracken, *Chairman, Council of Economic Advisers*

Robert Mayo, *Director, Bureau of the Budget*

Richard Nathan, *Assistant Director, Bureau of the Budget (human resources)*

Robert Ellsworth, *U.S. Ambassador to NATO*

PREFACE:
BETWEEN NIXON AND MOYNIHAN

I am the only person—perhaps in the world—who was a friend of both Richard Nixon and Daniel Patrick Moynihan before they knew each other.

The Professor and the President is the story of the consequences of their paths crossing in 1969, when a conservative president made a liberal professor his urban affairs adviser in the White House.

For Moynihan, this was a trajectory change that would lead ultimately to his becoming U.S. ambassador to India, appointed by Nixon; U.S. representative to the United Nations, appointed by President Gerald Ford, Nixon's successor; and through his celebrity at the UN to the U.S. Senate, where he was elected four times from New York.

For Nixon, it imbued his domestic policy with a progressive cast that he had neither promised nor imagined.

I FIRST MET Nixon just after he lost the presidency to John F. Kennedy in 1960 and returned to California. I had been a speechwriter for President Eisenhower from 1958 to 1961, when Nixon was vice president. Nixon was not a presence in the White House, because he didn't have an office like subsequent vice presidents. In fact, Eisenhower considered the vice presidency to be constitutionally part of the legislative branch.

When it was over, Eisenhower got in his old car and was driven the 80 miles home to Gettysburg, Pennsylvania. Ex-presidents then did not get the staff, offices, and other perks they now require. The Republican National Committee determined that to keep Ike "alive" politically, someone would have to answer his mail. The job that I accepted was to be piecework, paid so many cents per letter. We failed to anticipate the deluge: it seemed like every student in America wanted Ike's opinion on what was that year's national debate topic, others wanted something for their charity auctions or his autograph, and some just wanted to say hello. (These letters provided the windfall that allowed me to become an independent writer.)

Whenever I heard that a friend of Eisenhower had won an award, received an honorary degree, or had a marriage or death in the family, I would draft a letter for him to send along. Soon, people were telling me, "I got the nicest note from the General," as Ike liked to be called.

All this was arranged by Bryce Harlow, who had been chief congressional lobbyist in the Eisenhower White House and was now the go-between for everything Republican in Washington. He also instructed me to attend to any needs Nixon might have. Nixon was now a "rainmaker" for a Los Angeles law firm. He was proud to have considerable income for the first time and to be able to build a house in the Trousdale Estates neighborhood in Beverly Hills. But he was bored. "If I have to play golf one more time with Randolph Scott, I may go out of my mind," he once told me. He missed the political gossip that had fueled his Washington life since 1947. I tried to oblige by writing what amounted to a newsletter with a subscription list of one.

I did not actually meet Nixon in person until the spring of 1961 when he wanted help writing articles for the *Saturday Evening Post* and other publications. Visiting Washington, he borrowed a desk in the law office of Bill Rogers, who had been Eisenhower's attorney general. (This was in the days before a large L.A. law firm was expected to have a Washington office.) After we discussed the articles, he said, "Incidentally, don't send me those draft letters. I don't want to be one of those politicians who remember people's birthdays." A lesson learned: Eisenhower, the warrior, was a natural politician; Nixon, the politician, was not.

I also learned how comfortable it was to help Nixon on writing projects, which I continued to do for the next three years. Unlike many public figures, who seemed to resent having words written for them, Nixon admired writers. (He told me that writing *Six Crises*, his episodic and compelling account of his political career from the Alger Hiss case in 1948 through losing the presidency in 1960, was one of the most difficult tasks he ever attempted.) Moreover, he was excessively generous, often splitting large fees with me. I said he was paying me too much, and he was embarrassed. "I'd only have to give the money to the IRS." Much about Nixon, I learned, was different from his public persona.

IF MY FRIENDSHIP with Nixon was largely professional and political, with Moynihan it was neither. Pat and I had been socially connected by Arthur Goldberg, who as secretary of labor had been Pat's boss in the Kennedy administration and was a friend of my family. Goldberg, as was his style, had declared from on high that we were two young men who were going to be friends. He was right. Pat and I instantly liked each other and, when we both lived in Cambridge, Massachusetts, wanted to spend as much time together as possible.

And through the years the memories compound. . . . At the Moynihans' upstate New York farm in Pindars Corner, Pat declaims to our teenage children, pointing to a sumptuous vegetable patch, "Future Leaders of America, go forth and pick the corn for dinner!" . . . . Trapped in Washington on a boiling July Sunday, the new senator calls to propose a picnic! His secret is he has discovered a grotto on the Capitol grounds where the wine will stay cool—my wife, Beth, and I join Pat and his wife, Liz—as we will again years later in Istanbul and at the ruins of Ephesus to share their fortieth wedding anniversary.

After Pat's death in 2003, Liz said, "You loved him and he loved you." Was there anything of Pat's I'd like to have? "Three bow ties," I said. "But you don't wear bow ties." "Yes, but I will frame them and have them with me whenever I'm at home."

INTRODUCTION:
POLITICS MAKES STRANGE BEDFELLOWS

Many years ago in Washington I invented a Valentine's Day game that I called "Politics Makes Strange Bedfellows." A bowl filled with 50 names—male, female, living, dead, real, fictional—circles the table as the players draw names from it. The objective is to stop when you believe you have constructed the most outrageous or unique couple. Winning is always by consensus. The Marquis de Sade paired with Mother Teresa might be a contender, but would probably be rejected as too obvious. My friends were into subtlety and nuance.

Had we played our game on Valentine's Day 1969, Richard Milhous Nixon and Daniel Patrick Moynihan surely would have been debated with passion and dismissed as too improbable. Of all the odd couples in American public life, were they not the oddest?

Pat Moynihan famously told us that we are entitled to our own opinions, but not to our own facts. Yet writers must choose from a gallery of facts and arrange them in an order that best explains what they are trying to do. Take the subtitle of this study: it announces that I will be writing about a specific man, in a specific place, at a specific time, that is, Daniel Patrick Moynihan in the Nixon White House.

My first challenge is not to stray. Nixon and Moynihan, figures of historical dimension, must be contained in 1969–70, the two years that they are together in the White House. For instance, Watergate at that time is no more than a building complex in Foggy Bottom, of significance only in the real estate columns. Nixon, Moynihan, and the rest of us in this story do not know the future. If you do, please suspend memory to let our story reflect its own reality. This is what the writer is going to do—in the present tense—unless there is a reason for doing otherwise.

My second challenge is to stay focused. Nixon is always waiting in the wings to take command of a story. In 1994, 20 years after Nixon's resignation as president of the United States, I arranged a luncheon for filmmaker Oliver Stone. Stone wanted to introduce Anthony Hopkins, the British actor who would portray Nixon in Stone's upcoming movie, to four people who knew the president: press secretary Ron Ziegler, law partner Len Garment, political aide John Sears, and myself. At some point I whispered to Hopkins, "Listen, Tony, each one of us is describing a totally different person!" But Nixon's story must be resisted because this is Pat's story.

I will also work hard to stay out of the story as much as possible. The story is from my point of view, but it is not my story.

PART I

THE TRANSITION
NOVEMBER 1968 TO JANUARY 1969

WHY NIXON WANTS MOYNIHAN

On December 10, 1968, at Nixon's transition headquarters at the Pierre Hotel on New York's Fifth Avenue, the president-elect announces that Daniel Patrick Moynihan, 41, will join his White House staff as assistant to the president for urban affairs. Professor Moynihan will take a two-year leave from his position as director of the Joint Center for Urban Studies at Harvard University and the Massachusetts Institute of Technology. Nixon says that he will create by executive order a new council that will serve as a "domestic counterpart of the National Security Council."

In the next day's *Washington Post,* Bernard Nossiter describes Moynihan as "six foot, five inches of corrosive wit, infuriating candor, and towering intelligence." In the *New York Times,* R. W. Apple Jr. writes that Moynihan "will probably be the most visible Democrat in the new [Republican] Administration." Don Irwin, in the *Los Angeles Times,* notes that "Nixon and his new aide seemed to be leaning over backward during their informal press conference to avoid issues on which they have made conflicting statements in the past."

How did Moynihan come to be Nixon's Democrat?

The year 1969 is not a good one for a Republican to become president. Nixon is fully aware of the problems that can result from winning the presidency with a narrow plurality of the popular vote, as he will later acknowledge in his memoirs. (Nixon won 43.4 percent of the vote, barely edging out Democrat Hubert Humphrey's 42.7 percent. Independent candidate George Wallace polled 13.5 percent of the vote.) Nixon may or may not also be aware that the last new president to take office with both houses of Congress controlled by the opposition was Zachary Taylor—in 1848.

Appointing a prominent Democrat to his cabinet might help. It is a path full of precedent. On the eve of World War II, President Franklin D. Roosevelt, a Democrat, chose Republicans Henry L. Stimson and Frank Knox to be, respectively, his secretary of war and secretary of the navy. Republican president Dwight D. Eisenhower picked union leader Martin Durkin as his first secretary of labor. Democratic president John F. Kennedy reached out to satisfy Wall Street by appointing Douglas Dillon as his treasury secretary.

Nixon's first choice among Democrats to join his administration had been Henry "Scoop" Jackson, the strongly anti-communist senator from the state of Washington, for the defense post. Jackson wants the job, but declines under pressure from other Democratic senators. He reportedly tells Nixon's aides that liberal Democrats in the Senate would make his life miserable. Hubert Humphrey, the man Nixon has just defeated, is offered the United Nations ambassador post—but this is less a serious offer than a symbolic gesture of conciliation. Nixon next approaches Sargent Shriver, John F. Kennedy's brother-in-law, for the UN post. According to Nixon, Shriver replies that he would accept if the president-elect pledges not to cut federal poverty programs. Shriver is told that his demand is "intolerable."

Unmaking a cabinet officer is much easier than making one, as Eisenhower illustrated when he eased union leader Durkin out of his conservative government with thanks for his "unique value." But a White House staff job—close to the president, with responsibility for proposing and formulating policy—is a politically risky place to put a Democrat like Moynihan, who had been an author of the anti-poverty programs that Nixon had attacked during his campaign. Moreover, there is no personal history between them. Nixon doesn't know Moynihan; he even asks a young campaign worker, Chris DeMuth, who had gone to Harvard, whether Pat is called "Daniel or Dan."

Moynihan's name is raised immediately after the election, recalled speechwriter Bill Safire, to which Nixon asks, "But could we count on him to be loyal? I don't mean Republican. I mean—you know—one of us."

Moynihan will later say, "I got my job in the Nixon administration as the result of a speech." The speech, in September 1967, was titled "The Politics of Stability." Nixon had moved to New York after his failed campaign for governor of California, and Leonard Garment, his new law partner, called Moynihan's remarks to his attention. Moynihan "proposed that American politics were approaching instability, and that liberals who understood this should seek out and make alliances with their conservative equivalents in order to preserve democratic institutions from the looming forces of the authoritarian left and right." Moynihan was for a policy of sharing federal money with state and local governments. Washington is "good at collecting revenues and rather bad at disbursing services."

As for urban riots that had rocked the country in the mid-1960s, the cities erupted "in the aftermath of one of the most extraordinary periods of liberal electoral victories that we have ever experienced. Who are [liberals], then, to be pointing fingers?" Moynihan concluded, "The politics of stability are not at first exciting. It is only when we come to see how very probably our national life is at stake that the game acquires a sudden interest." Thus, Moynihan's ideas about the failures of 1960s liberalism came to be echoed in Nixon's December 1967 address to the National Association of Manufacturers in New York City. Garment remembers, "Big speech, black tie, Waldorf. He gets a standing ovation, which is not something that Nixon is getting at that time."

If Nixon wants a Democrat, Pat wants a president.

WHY MOYNIHAN WANTS NIXON

f Nixon choosing Pat is a politically difficult decision, Pat joining Nixon is a psychologically vexing one. For a coming-of-age East Coast liberal, the defining image of Nixon—immortalized in a 1954 Herblock cartoon—is a swarthy, bare knuckle campaigner coming up from the sewer.

Pat is the young man seeking a career in public service: first work for a candidate—W. Averell Harriman for governor of New York—and when Harriman wins in 1954, Pat goes to Albany as assistant to the secretary to the governor. He is successful, moving up to assistant secretary and, later, acting secretary to the governor. Next on to Washington: John F. Kennedy is elected president in 1960, and Pat becomes special assistant to the secretary of labor, then executive assistant to the secretary of labor, and then assistant secretary of labor. Each job a step up.

Labor is not a top-tier agency, like State, Defense, Treasury, and Justice. But Pat has a remarkable talent for expanding his jurisdiction. His boss, Labor Secretary Arthur Goldberg, wants a new building for his department and has his assistant draft a "Report to the President by the Ad Hoc Committee on Federal Office Space." The subject is office space, not architecture, yet Pat tacks on his "Guiding Principles for Federal Architecture," which will become the U.S. government's policy on the architecture of federal buildings. His grand proposal calls for the redevelopment of Pennsylvania Avenue, the immense thoroughfare between the Capitol and the White House. President Kennedy likes the idea; Pat then puts together an informal group to draw up the plan.

He is a 38-year-old assistant secretary of labor when, in March 1965, he writes a government report that describes a strange pattern he has noticed in the country's economic data. From the end of World War II through the early 1960s, whenever black male unemployment rises, so too do new welfare cases. Then, suddenly, unemployment goes down but welfare cases continue to go up. Could this be reflecting a new form of urban underclass?

The 78 pages of statistics, graphs, and tables in "The Negro Family: The Case for National Action," along with some dramatic phrases about a "tangle of pathology," trace the deterioration of lower-class black family life in the inner cities. It becomes known as the "Moynihan Report" after it is leaked in August. (Also in August there are six days of large-scale rioting in Watts, a predominantly black area of Los Angeles, set off by a white highway patrolman arresting a young black motorist.) Pat means his research "to start a serious conversation among policymakers and to prod government officials into devising far-reaching socioeconomic reforms," according to historian James T. Patterson. Instead, he is attacked as a racist, smearing black culture and "blaming the victim." James Farmer, head of the Congress of Racial Equality, declares, "We are sick unto death of being analyzed, mesmerized, bought, sold, and slobbered over, while the same evils that are the ingredients of our oppression go unattended."

The angry reaction to the report among liberals turns its author into an embarrassment for the national Democratic Party. He becomes a nonperson in Lyndon Johnson's Washington as well as on the Upper West Side of Manhattan. "The people you would most want to admire you [are] detesting you," he later tells an interviewer from the *New York Times*. Pat returns to New York in July 1965 to run in the Democratic Party primary for president of the City Council and loses in September.

Pat turns to life in the academy. *Time* puts him on the cover of its July 28, 1967, issue. The article inside describes him as a "historian by training, sociologist by bent, politician by inclination, and intellectual gadfly by design." Still, he admits to being "distressed not to have any influence on anybody" in Washington. Perhaps if Robert F. Kennedy is elected president in 1968, he will gain reentry in national affairs. Pat campaigns for Kennedy in California. But Kennedy is assassinated in Los Angeles on the day he wins the state's Democratic primary. He writes Ted Kennedy, "I loved Bob," yet in the letter (which he does not send) he also worries that Bob was losing sight of "the people of South Boston and Dorchester" in favor of "the salons of Central Park West."

Pat endorses his party's nominee, Hubert Humphrey, for whom he has personal affection. Yet in September he writes Harry McPherson, President Johnson's counsel, "There are a great many people like me who in all realism could only expect that a Humphrey victory will mean that the persons who have so assiduously kept us out of influence in these recent years will be continued in power."

Humphrey doesn't win. Instead, the man of whom left-wing editor Victor Navasky declaims, "You can't have voted for Richard Nixon and be a member of the New York intellectual establishment," invites Pat back into Washington's power center.

THE COURTSHIP

The first step in Nixon's courtship of Pat Moynihan comes when his inner circle turns to thinking of possibilities for the cabinet. Pat's most enthusiastic advocate is Bob Finch, whom Nixon is going to make secretary of health, education, and welfare. Another supporter, Len Garment, recalls the success of Moynihan's ideas in Nixon's speech on the failures of 1960s liberalism. Bob Haldeman, the president-elect's chief of staff, tells Garment, "Nixon wants you to sound out Moynihan to see if he's interested in coming into the administration. But if so, doing what, where?" Garment calls him and they agree to meet at the Laurent Restaurant in New York City. "It was a fine dinner," Garment recalls. "A lot of fun, a lot of laughter, very relaxed. Two bottles of Beaujolais. We don't want the table to be empty at any given moment."

Finally, Garment asks, "What would you want to do?"

"Transportation," replies Moynihan.

Moynihan's interest in transportation is not widely known—so his response is ostensibly surprising. However, in 1963 Pat had brought a young Ralph Nader into the Labor

Department to work on auto safety, a match that was to have international consequences. Pat told Garment he had been thinking about the significance of the interstate highway system, which then was barely a decade old, how it had changed America: American life, industry, communications. He saw all kinds of interesting possibilities, ways of spending money that would lead to jobs and so forth.

"That can't be," says Garment. "We're committed to Volpe, so it's got to be something else." John Volpe, the Republican governor of Massachusetts, had been considered as Nixon's running mate during the campaign.

"Well," replies Pat, "I'd like to have the urban equivalent of Henry Kissinger's job on the National Security Council. A National Urban Council or whatever the name will be."

Back in Cambridge, Pat calls me to say that Nixon wants to see him in New York. They have never met. Despite my friendships with Nixon and Moynihan, I have never recommended one to the other (although when the Nixon biography that I wrote with Earl Mazo came out before the 1968 election, I sent Moynihan a copy inscribed, "To Pat, In case you choose to hedge your bets").

I fly to New York to join Pat after he meets Nixon at the Pierre Hotel, the site of Nixon's transition headquarters. Pat comes into the dining room almost exploding with first impressions. He is excited by Nixon's offer of a White House position with a broad mandate. But what Pat can't get over is what the president-elect admits he doesn't know about the domestic policies of his country. "He's ignorant! He doesn't know anything." Pat chuckles, "I would have bluffed it."

But what Pat mistakes for ignorance is actually disinterest. This was something made clear to me on Election Day 1962, when

Nixon was running for governor of California and I was his speechwriter. I was returning home to Washington the next day when Nixon called me to say goodbye. At some point, I asked, "Do you still think you're going to lose the race, Dick?"

"Yes," he said. "But at least I'll never have to talk about crap like dope addiction again."

Dope addiction for Nixon was a local issue. What consumed Nixon was the world outside the United States and what America's place should be in it. During my years of helping him, we never had a single discussion on domestic issues, with the possible exception of crime. He had little interest in California issues, even while seeking the governorship. His Democratic opponent, Pat Brown, kept repeating that Sacramento was Nixon's stepping-stone to run again for the presidency in 1964. This was mildly ironic, because a principal reason Nixon ran for governor was to have an excuse not to run again against Kennedy. The political logic was that if Nixon couldn't win when Kennedy was a backbench senator in 1960, what chance would he have when Kennedy was president?

This is the odd condition of Richard Nixon: a man who so obsessively wanted to be president of the United States did not wish to involve himself in questions of its domestic governance. Will this have consequences now that he is to be president? Turning to Pat presents intriguing possibilities: (a) Nixon, ignorant of urban affairs, but to be tutored by a great teacher, will produce creative new policies; or (b) Nixon, consumed by international affairs, will stay away from urban problems, resulting in leaderless stasis; or (c) Nixon, without knowledge of urban affairs, relying on an adviser of a different political persuasion, will create confusion and recrimination in the government.

There is little doubt that Pat wants the job. The White House will always be the center of the political world, his world. And the world is in dangerous trouble. But Pat must first convince Liz, who has the best political instincts in the family and is not happy with her husband acquiring a Nixon connection. Pat makes the case that a president's offer of a serious assignment at a terrible time must be respected. Liz decides to stay in Cambridge with their three children; she reasons that if things do not go well for Pat in Washington, the escape back to Harvard will be less painful. In practice, this also means that Pat can do Herculean labor Monday through Friday in Washington with recuperative time in Cambridge on the weekend.

The announcement of Pat's appointment comes a week and a day after Nixon names Kissinger his assistant for national security. With this, the president-elect gives the two key substantive jobs in his White House to professors from Harvard, where, as Kissinger writes, "the faculty disdain for Richard Nixon was established orthodoxy" and where Nixon's feelings about "Harvard bastards" are equally explicit.

There is still more in the résumés of Nixon's two new aides that can hardly have escaped Nixon's notice or those in the media who have been psychoanalyzing him for at least a decade. Besides the Harvard connection, there is Nelson Rockefeller and John Kennedy. One is the Republican who always seems to be standing in Nixon's way. In 1960, before being able to accept the Republican Party's nomination, Nixon had to go hat-in-hand to Rockefeller's apartment in New York City to accept changes in the party platform. The other is the Democrat who swiped the presidency from him in 1960, with the tainted help of Richard Daley in Chicago and Lyndon Johnson in Texas.

Pat Moynihan is emotionally connected to the Kennedys. A generation in Washington still remembers how, on the death of JFK, columnist Mary McGrory said to him, "We'll never laugh again," to which he replied, "We'll laugh again. It's just we'll never be young again." Henry Kissinger is even more firmly connected to Nelson Rockefeller, "the single most influential person in my life," to whose memory he will dedicate the memoirs of his years with President Nixon.

The Harvards, the Kennedys, Nelson Rockefeller all represent those whom Richard Nixon feels slighted or ignored by, even when he is the vice president of the United States—all those of the best butter, superior in breeding, who know which fork to use and consider him rancid. It is true that one of his "Harvard professors" had shined shoes on New York's 42nd Street, and the other had escaped Hitler's Germany. Yet for a shining moment in the life of Richard Milhous Nixon, he can raise high a middle finger at the establishment.

More significant is that the president-elect is now, at the outset of his presidency, prepared to reach out for advice from those of an intellectual weight that have never before been in his inner circle.

THE MEMORANDA

Nixon has barely finished announcing the Moynihan appointment when Pat's memoranda begin cascading onto his desk. The standard internal "Memorandum for the President," as I remember from my days in the Eisenhower White House, is kept to a page, if possible. The president is a busy man, as are his staffers.

But Pat's memos are long, at times very long, complicated, often convoluted. His style borders on the literary, more like essays, with a tad of the Britishisms he acquired when studying at the London School of Economics, filled with tasty quotations and arcane references. They are often about subjects, such as Negro-Jewish relations, that fascinate Pat and, in his opinion, should fascinate the president as well, even if they are outside presidential powers.

I don't think this is a strategy, at least not at first. It's just Pat being Pat, saying all the things he wants to say to a president if he ever has a chance. Nixon is meeting Pat through the memoranda, his introduction to a man he had not known and yet is elevating to a position of great importance to him and his government.

On January 9, 1969, Pat writes to Nixon:

In the months ahead I will be harassing you with details of the "urban crisis." Whatever the urgency of the matters I bring before you, I will be doing so in an essentially optimistic posture, which is to say that I will routinely assume that our problems are manageable if only we will manage them. This is the only position possible for government. Yet, of course, it does not necessarily reflect reality. It may be that our problems are not manageable, or that we are not capable of summoning the effort required to respond effectively. It seems to me important that you know that there are responsible persons who are very near to just that conclusion. (To be sure, twenty years ago in many scientific/academic circles it was taken as settled that the world would shortly blow itself up, yet we are still here.)

I had thought to summarize the views of the apocalyptic school, ranging in style as it does from the detached competence of Lewis Mumford who for forty years had foretold the approach of "Necropolis," the City of the Dead, all the way to the more hysterical members of the New Left who assume that the only thing that can save this civilization is for it to be destroyed. However, I have just come upon a document of careful men who recently met to discuss the state of New York City. I am associated with a quarterly journal, The Public Interest, *which is devoting a special issue to New York. On December 17 we assembled a group of city officials and similarly informed persons for a day-long session at the Century Club. (I could not be present owing to my new assignment.) Paul Weaver, a young assistant professor of government at Harvard, attended as a kind of rapporteur. Later he summarized his impression of the meeting in terms that seem to me persuasive, and as he himself put it, "not a little chilling."*

His central point—an immensely disturbing one—is that the
social system of American and British democracy that grew up in
the eighteenth and nineteenth centuries was able to be exceedingly
permissive with regard to public matters precisely because it could
depend on its citizens to be quite disciplined with respect to private
ones. He speaks of "private sub-systems of authority," such as the
family, church, and local community, and political party, which reg-
ulated behavior, instilled motivation, etc., in such a way as to make
it unnecessary for the State to intervene in order to protect "the
public interest." More and more it would appear these subsystems
are breaking down in the immense city of New York. If this should
continue, democracy would break down.

Most staff memos to a president are essentially politician-to-
politician or expert-to-CEO. But Pat is writing to Nixon *intellectual-
to-intellectual,* without a bit of patronizing. Nixon has never been
treated this way before. He loves it!

Now that he is finally to be president, Nixon seems to have
room for knowledge other than what he has needed to get there.
And for Pat, the professor, there is the delighted discovery that his
student is very bright and easy to engage.

JANUARY 15, 1969
TO: BOB HALDEMAN
FROM: RN

The Moynihan memorandum of January 9 on urban problems
should be made available to the research team and to the Cabinet members who are on the Urban Affairs Council. It should be
emphasized in distributing this memorandum and others like it,
which will be coming in, that this is not a final policy paper but
the kind of incisive and stimulating analysis which I think should

constantly be brought to the attention of policymakers. Be sure also that Garment gets a copy of this memorandum and of others like it in the future.

The president's practice of sharing Pat's memos throughout his government almost guarantees that eventually there will be an embarrassing leak. But that leak—which will outrage the civil rights movement, embarrass the administration, and prompt Pat to offer his resignation—won't happen for another year.

NIXON: "THE DURABLE MAN"

How could Richard Nixon have become president with a domestic policy that is primarily a collection of boiler-plate statements put out by the campaign, usually not even spoken by the candidate himself?

For example, consider this statement released by the Nixon-Agnew Campaign Committee on July 6, 1968: "Before new economic resources are committed to the cities, they must receive an infusion of the nation's best intellectual resources, drawn not only from the government and the academic community, but also from the relatively untapped business and financial community. In the last century, men of action built the cities. In the next stage of America's urban growth, men of thought and action must use new ideas to rebuild the cities."

The difference in the quality of Nixon's domestic and foreign pronouncements is stark. When he asks Kissinger to take the National Security Council job, he urges him first to read an article he wrote for *Foreign Affairs* ("Asia after Viet Nam," October 1967), in which he hints at what will become his famous opening to China. But what can he offer Pat to read?

Why doesn't Nixon have a body of thought on domestic issues similar to what he has developed on foreign policy?

On the eve of the 1968 presidential election year, David Broder and I wrote *The Republican Establishment* (Harper & Row, 1967), a can't-tell-the-players-without-a-scorecard book in which we described the political Nixon as he looked to us at about the time Pat first met him. The book followed Nixon's career through an ever-widening trail of political campaigns. We called Nixon "The Durable Man"—congressman at 33, important congressman at 35 (after his role in the Alger Hiss case), senator at 37, vice president at 39, reelected vice president at 43, unsuccessful candidate for president at 47, candidate for governor of California at 49. But this was a bare outline.

When not campaigning for himself, Nixon campaigned for others, notably every other year for congressional candidates. As Nixon said in 1964, "I want all Republicans to win; I am just as strong for a liberal Republican in New York as I am for a conservative Republican in Texas, and I can go and just as enthusiastically campaign for both." For Nixon, the end that justified these means was "the incomparable power of the presidency." And in a presidential nominating system that was then more determined by Republican loyalists at county and state conventions than by a broader based electorate voting in state primaries, Nixon would be there whenever a Republican needed help.

Once, over a three-hour period, we watched Nixon campaign with equal conviction for staunch conservative congressional candidate Donald E. Lukens in Ohio and liberal congressional candidate Fred Schwengel in Iowa, both of whom would win their seats. How could Nixon—who would need the support of Lukens and Schwengel to get the Republican nomination—have a domestic policy that satisfied them both?

Nixon once told me about working through a steamy North Carolina summer for a professor at Duke when he was a student in the law school, hand-cranking an inky mimeograph machine eight hours a day in an airless cubicle. It was the worst job of his life, but he was doing whatever was necessary to supplement his scholarship. His point was that the end justified the means. Not having a domestic policy is a means if the end is winning the support of enough Lukens and Schwengel Republicans.

Yet candidates make alterations after they get the nomination. Nixon might have had a domestic policy in 1968 if he had needed one to help get elected. Campaigns are often where proposals, policies, and programs are invented. But his strategy—strictly enforced by campaign manager John Mitchell—was not to distract voters with issues. The presidential election of 1968 was a "throw the bums out" election. Public displeasure with the Vietnam War and urban street riots would be sufficient to win.

So when Pat joins Nixon at the White House in 1969, the president can offer him a unique gift: a clean slate to write upon.

PART II

A YEAR OF TURMOIL
1969

A FULL AGENDA

Preparing his new boss to be president of the United States, Pat sends a memo on January 3 outlining "the two most conspicuous" policy challenges the president will be confronting in the new year: "the Negro revolution and the war in Vietnam." Pat is a fervent critic of the war, yet his understanding with Nixon is to refrain from public comment while in the White House. However, he cannot resist privately reminding him from time to time that the war is a "disaster," and how much the money could be better spent.

Pat writes Nixon, "Fifteen blocks or so from the White House is a corridor of burned out, boarded up shops on 14th Street which for practical purposes are today in precisely the condition they were left two days after the April [1968] riots" that followed the assassination of Martin Luther King Jr. "It would be difficult to find a more depressing sight."

He urges an early presidential visit to the riot corridors that can symbolically show Nixon's concern. So in his second week in office, on January 31, the president stands in front of the gutted Waxie Maxie record store on 7th Street NW and announces that a vest-pocket park will be built on the site of four burned-out buildings. The idea for the park, Pat recalls, came to him on "a trip to Detroit after Christmas" when he saw that "save for one or two such parks, the commercial strips remain pretty much in the ruined condition they were left in 18 months ago." (Followed by bureaucratic bumbling, lack of money, and other distractions, January 31 represents the high point of the administration's Washington rebuilding efforts.)

But 1969 will not follow the arc of 1968. It is not going to be another year of summer rioting in the inner city. Blacks see their destroyed neighborhoods and local businesses less as a forward advance than as a terrible setback. Moreover, it is soon clear that the national civil rights leaders are in the midst of their own internal disputes.

The massive protests of 1969 will take place on college campuses rather than in the ghettos. At the White House, Pat's young staff will meticulously pinpoint the paths of the campus uprisings, starting at the great universities on the East and West coasts, traveling inland in all directions, a contagion moving from large schools to small schools, private and public, until the entire map is covered with their pins: San Francisco State (January 6), Brandeis (January 8), Swarthmore (January 9), Berkeley (February 4), University of Wisconsin (February 12), City College of New York (February 13), Duke (February 13), Rutgers (February 24).

On April 9, Harvard students take over University Hall. A few minutes before 5 a.m. the next morning, police in riot helmets break through the doors with a three-foot battering ram, club the occupiers, and leave Harvard Yard around 6 a.m. The cause of the protests, as Professor John Kenneth Galbraith will later recall, "was Vietnam, only and always Vietnam."

The exceptions to this rule are the April 19 and 20 protests at Cornell, where the demands of a group of mostly black students relate to campus racism, not Vietnam. Negotiations to end the students' occupation of Willard Straight Hall are complicated by the radical Students for a Democratic Society (SDS). The photograph of African American students with rifles and bandoliers leaving Straight Hall will win a Pulitzer Prize—and a place in Vice President Spiro Agnew's attacks on student protesters who "have never done a productive thing in their lives."

While students have an assortment of education demands—curricula reform, a larger role in campus decisionmaking, dropping compulsory ROTC requirements—Vietnam is their overwhelming, overriding concern. The antiwar movement is more than a youth crusade. But young people are the ones being sent to Vietnam, where the military casualties keep mounting. Forty thousand had died by the end of 1968, and nearly 12,000 more will die in 1969. Pat's staff and other young White House aides keep up a steady conversation with student groups. Marty Anderson, who had been a research director in Nixon's campaign, keeps pressing for an all-volunteer army. The administration is listening, but has little more to offer than threadbare suggestions for more advisory committees and youth appointments.

On August 19, Pat writes to Nixon:

So long as the Vietnam war continues, student protest constitutes an immediate and direct threat to the day-to-day effectiveness of the national government, quite apart from any long range concerns.

I would expect there will be considerable anti-war protest in the coming academic year. . . . I am not sure what you can do about all this. Except of course to end the war, which is precisely your desire

*and intent. But to do so successfully imposes restraints on what
you can say in public so great that I would imagine there cannot be
much successful dialogue between the students and the Administration on this issue per se.*

On October 15, protesters stage a day of nationwide demon-
strations calling for a "moratorium" on the war. A quarter of a
million people assemble outside the White House. The next day
the president asks for staff assessments. Pat replies:

> The Moratorium was a success. *It was not perhaps as big as some
> may have anticipated—"substantial but not enormous," in David
> Brinkley's words—but in style and content it was everything the
> organizers could have hoped for. The young white middle class
> crowds were sweet-tempered and considerate: at times even radi-
> ant. (Really. The only term by which to describe the march past the
> White House is joyous.) The movement lost no friends. It gained, I
> should think, a fair number of recruits and a great deal of prestige.*

The demonstrators had their own marshals to ensure that the
peace march would indeed be peaceful, and the administration
assigned people to be in touch with them, including Pat's young
assistants Dick Blumenthal and Checker Finn. Years later, Pat
will recall the moment for his friend Nat Glazer: "They did a first-
rate job, but [John] Mitchell got carried away: 'It looks like the
Russian Revolution,' was his famous summation, gazing down
from the Attorney General's office. At one point he became con-
vinced that Blumenthal was in cahoots with the demonstrators
and had him removed from his post. [Blumenthal] was certain
he was going to be fired, and I was pretty sure an attempt would
be made. I told him . . . simply to do nothing and we would let

Mitchell find out that there were limits to his power: if Blumenthal went, so would I have done, and in the end nothing happened."

On November 15, at the next moratorium protest, the crowd in Washington reaches 300,000. About 40,000 participate in a silent "march of death," carrying placards bearing the names of Americans killed in Vietnam as they walk past the White House. On the National Mall, Pete Seeger sings John Lennon's new song: "Give Peace a Chance." Thousands of protesters take up the song. After each verse, Seeger shouts, "Are you listening, Pentagon? Are you listening, Agnew? Are you listening, Nixon?"

As 1969 comes to an end, the president announces that he has withdrawn more than 100,000 troops from Vietnam in the eleven months since his inauguration on January 20. The total number of troops still in Vietnam is 434,000.

INAUGURATION DAY: JANUARY 20

The day, writes *New York Times* columnist Russell Baker, is "out of Edgar Allan Poe, dun and drear, with a chilling northeast wind that cut to the marrow, and a gray ugly overcast that turned the city the color of wet cement." The president-elect is wearing a morning coat and striped pants, his right hand is on the family Bible, open to Isaiah 2:4: "They shall beat their swords into plowshares, and their spears into pruning hooks: nation shall not lift up sword against nation, neither shall they learn war any more."

His friend Arthur Burns writes in his diary, "I had never seen eyes sparkle so. . . . [For a man] wanting fiercely to be president . . . [it is] a moment of triumph and fulfillment."

Nixon repeats the oath of office as read to him by Chief Justice Earl Warren: "I, Richard Milhous Nixon, do solemnly swear that I will faithfully execute the Office of President of the United States, and will to the best of my ability, preserve, protect and defend the Constitution of the United States." For the first time, "Hail to the Chief" is being played for him. In the distance, a twenty-one-gun salute is fired from howitzers of the Military District of Washington. Later in the day, he will be given the card that unlocks the nuclear code.

The president's address takes seventeen minutes (longer than Kennedy's, but not too long). He avoids the major themes of the campaign—law and order and civil disobedience—instead stressing reconciliation both at home and abroad:

> We are caught in war, wanting peace. We are torn by division, wanting unity. We see around us empty lives, wanting fulfillment. We see tasks that need doing, waiting for hands to do them. To a crisis of the spirit, we need an answer of the spirit. And to find that answer, we need only look within ourselves. . . .
>
> To lower our voices would be a simple thing. In these difficult years, America has suffered from a fever of words; from inflated rhetoric that promises more than it can deliver; from angry rhetoric that fans discontents into hatreds; from bombastic rhetoric that postures instead of persuading. We cannot learn from one another until we stop shouting at one another—until we speak quietly enough so that our words can be heard as well as our voices.

The muted tone is appreciated by the media. Liberal columnist Joseph Kraft notes that the new president emphasized words like "together" and "negotiations," concluding, "Mr. Nixon, in sum, was speaking in homilies. But he had the right homilies for the moment."

WHILE THE NIXON team spends the transition at the Pierre Hotel in New York City, Pat has moved to Washington, where he can work out of the offices of the Pennsylvania Avenue Commission. He is vice chairman. His 1963 proposal to President Kennedy for recreating Pennsylvania Avenue is now a work-in-progress.

For sleeping and dining, he borrows the Georgetown home of his former boss, Averell Harriman. It comes complete with staff and wine cellar. Pat writes Harriman, who is in Paris as a U.S. representative to the Vietnam peace talks, "I have finally had the chance really to *look* at those impressionists. Always before one walked into the room, recognizing a Cezanne and a Van Gogh much as one recognized other people in the room, but never having the opportunity to stare unabashedly." He adds, "I will get out the moment of your return." (Pat's perfect "thank you" gift is a necktie decorated with crocodiles. "The Crocodile" is Harriman's code name in confidential diplomatic cables, honoring his toughness as a negotiator.)

Pat's most urgent task is to assemble a staff. He asks me to join him, which results in Nixon appointing me deputy assistant to the president for urban affairs. As Pat's senior staff member, my job is primarily trying to maintain enough order so that we all know— at the same time, if possible—what Pat is asking each of us to do. I will also fill in for Pat when he cannot be someplace ("someplace" being a department meeting or a speaking date in Boston or Hong Kong). In baseball terms, I will be Pat's "bench coach," helping to strategize as Pat steps into a new Republican league.

A lot of valuable people—White House fellows, interns, others detailed from the civil service, academics on brief assignment— will be attached to the Moynihan office. Story Zartman, Pat's buddy from the Navy and now an attorney for Eastman Kodak, helps out for a couple of months until being appointed general counsel of the Small Business Administration. Michael Monroe, from the campaign, is also a staff assistant until he moves to the White House Conference on Food, Nutrition and Health.

But in the day-in, day-out, fifteen-hour days, six-day work weeks, the heavy lifting will be done by four incredibly smart and dedicated young men: Richard Blumenthal (22), Christopher DeMuth (22), Chester "Checker" E. Finn Jr. (25), and John R. Price (30). Dick and Checker were Pat's students at Harvard. Chris and John came from the campaign. Many years later, when he is no longer a young man, Chris DeMuth will tell an interviewer that Washington is a town run by "unqualified young people who just happen to be standing around at the right time. In politics, the hierarchy gets swept away every four, six, or eight years." (What becomes of Pat's young men after their years in the Nixon White House will be told in the afterword.)

AS THE INAUGURAL parade moves down Pennsylvania Avenue from the Capitol to the White House, it is interrupted in places by antiwar protesters. But for most Americans the parade represents the peaceful transfer of political power in a democracy from one party to another. My family and I watch the parade from our seats in front of the White House. Afterward, I take my sons, Charles and James, into the West Wing basement to show them my new office. Jamie, a few days past his fifth birthday, looks the place over. He concludes, "Not bad, Daddy, not bad."

NIXON'S TEAM OF RIVALS

On January 21, Nixon's first full day on the job, Dr. Arthur Burns, a trusted friend of the president from their years together in the Eisenhower administration, arrives in the Oval Office. He is there to give the president a report on proposed actions he has culled from the volunteer task forces he supervised during the transition. According to his diary, "The Pres. glanced over it, then proceeded to describe my new job. I just gasped. I had expressed disinclination previously to a W.H. post. I still felt that way, and wanted to protest—to plead a misunderstanding. But the Pres. did not give me a chance to plead or explain. He just smiled, waved aside my inarticulate but perfectly clear reluctance to take the post."

Immediately after the election in November, Nixon had asked Burns to join the White House staff. The offer, as Burns remembered, was to be something like a domestic czar, akin to Kissinger's role in foreign policy. But Burns was looking forward to a year in California and hoped to return to Washington only when the Federal Reserve chairmanship became available in January 1970. So he declined Nixon's offer. Had his decision been otherwise, Nixon gladly would have turned over his domestic agenda to Burns, and the first year of the Nixon administration would rate "Traditional Republican," no surprises, mostly budget balancing in keeping with Nixon's characterization of himself as a "moderate conservative."

Instead, the day after his January 21 meeting with Burns, Nixon signs his first executive order establishing the Council for Urban Affairs (UAC) with Daniel P. Moynihan as executive secretary. Ever since Pat's appointment in December, the press has been reporting that Nixon is giving "Dr. Moynihan authority in the domestic field comparable to Dr. Henry Kissinger in the national security field." In which case, what role is the president carving out for Burns?

Washington doesn't have to wait long for the answer. On January 23, the White House press office issues the following statement by the president: "Today I am pleased to announce a major appointment. Dr. Arthur Burns, a longtime friend and trusted adviser, has agreed to join the White House Staff as the Counsellor to the President. Dr. Burns will have Cabinet rank. He will head up a small group whose prime responsibility will be the coordination of the development of my domestic policies and programs." The announcement also says that his deputy will be Martin Anderson, 32, a Ph.D. from MIT, who had been a research director in the campaign.

Ten years later, Nixon will explain in his memoirs, "I thought that [Burns's] conservatism would be a useful and creative counterweight to Moynihan's liberalism." As with all presidential memoirs, this could be part of the process of tidying history. The most likely reason for choosing Burns and Moynihan is that neither Nixon nor his chief of staff, Bob Haldeman, have given any serious thought to the consequences. The ten-week transition is always an exhausting and confusing experience for a president-elect and his inner circle.

At any rate, Burns is surprised—and Pat is surprised. Perhaps Nixon is also surprised. A system of multiple advocacy is a recognized and respected type of management. But there is nothing Hegelian in Nixon's nature or his management practices up to this time. This was not how he ran the vice president's office or his campaigns. His habit was to place aides in distinct, noncompetitive boxes, creating smooth one-on-one relationships with those in his inner circle. Moreover, he has made clear to others that as president he plans to follow a modified Eisenhower model. Eisenhower was well known for clearly separating his streams of advice.

It is expected—some say "promised"—that Nixon will make Burns the Fed chairman when William McChesney Martin's term ends. Nixon may simply want to take advantage of Burns's talents in the meantime or to bestow an interim reward on a friend—in which case the implications of multiple advocacy are far from his mind.

Arthur Burns, now 65 years old, was brought to the United States from Austria when he was 10 years old. A distinguished professor of economics at Columbia University, he has known Nixon since 1953, when Nixon was vice president and Burns was Eisenhower's chairman of the Council of Economic Advisers. Although Eisenhower held Burns in the highest regard, Burns could not convince him to cut taxes as a stimulus during the 1958 recession. Eisenhower was more concerned with inflation. It was a debate that would have an important impact on the 1960 presidential election: if the recovery had come earlier in 1960, it might have helped Nixon prevail over Kennedy in November.

"Unfortunately," as Nixon wrote in *Six Crises,* "Arthur Burns turned out to be a good prophet. The bottom of the 1960 dip did come in October and the economy started to move up again in November—after it was too late to affect the election returns." Such support is not something that Nixon will forget.

Now, as president, Nixon sets up—deliberately or accidentally—a perfect intellectual storm at the center of his government. Two Ivy League heavyweights: on the left, Daniel Patrick Moynihan, Harvard; on the right, Arthur Burns, Columbia. Even their scholarly disciplines—Moynihan, the sociologist; Burns, the economist—guarantee very different approaches. "Burns was a specialist with specific ideas on economic policy. Moynihan, as a public intellectual, had opinions on everything," notes Tevi Troy in his exceptional little book *Intellectuals and the American Presidency* (Rowman & Littlefield, 2002). "When faced with a problem, Burns suggested answers; Moynihan suggested looking at the causes behind the problems." The pair could produce a great debate at any faculty club—but how would that debate play out in the White House?

In the White House version of the rock-paper-scissors game, however, virtually all the advantages appear to be with Burns: Burns's cabinet rank covers Moynihan's position of senior staff. Burns's "domestic affairs" mandate covers Moynihan's "urban affairs." Burns is a Republican and an old friend of the president; Moynihan is neither. Burns is conservative; Moynihan liberal (and Nixon is more conservative than liberal).

Still, Moynihan has one advantage. The dynamic of a White House does not live by status alone, nor even by substance. Sometimes it needs style.

Burns is boring—a fact recognized by anyone who has to wait for his words to emerge as he pulls on his pipe. Pat's quick wit is immediately appreciated by the gray suits that are now his White House colleagues. There is "a gala air about Pat, as though he was on his way to the circus," recalls an old friend. Peter Flanigan, Wall Street's representative on the staff, tells me, "It wouldn't be as much fun without him."

When the staff secretary asks Pat for his recommendation on a proposed presidential Message to Congress on Obscenity, he replies, "As you know, instead of sending to the Congress a Message on Obscenity, I have been in favor of sending them a dirty movie."

The two domestic advisers will soon run up against the constraints imposed by the president's priorities. In a sense, their real rival is Henry Kissinger. Even beyond the massive concerns of fighting and ending the Vietnam War, there is Nixon's abiding fascination with the geopolitics of the world.

Barely a month in office, Nixon and Kissinger are off on a "European Journey"—as chronicled in Kissinger's memoirs—to explore the "Malaise of the Western Alliance" . . . NATO in Brussels . . . London and the "Special Relationship" . . . Berlin and "The Enigma of Germany" . . . "Rome Interlude" . . . "The Colossus of de Gaulle." The president's daily diary provides a minute-by-minute account: "Met with the Prime Minister . . . motored to Chequers . . . flew to Bonn . . . motored to German Chancellery . . . motored to Quai d'Orsay . . . motored to Vatican." On other journeys in 1969, Nixon and Kissinger travel to Montreal, Manila, Jakarta, Bangkok, Saigon, New Delhi, and Lahore.

When Nixon accepted the presidential nomination in Miami, in August 1968, he spoke of himself as the child who "hears a train go by at night and he dreams of faraway places where he'd like to go." When he arrives in Bucharest, Romania, in August, Nixon becomes the first American president to pay a state visit to a communist country. The *New York Times* reports that the president receives an enthusiastic reception from hundreds of thousands of Romanians, many waving little American flags. At a folk dancing school, Nixon joins in a dance with Romanian president Nicolae Ceausescu, proving the political adage that there's no better way to lift the spirits of an American chief executive than by a well-planned visit to a carefully selected overseas location.

AT WORK IN THE
WEST WING BASEMENT

The West Wing administration of TV's Josiah Bartlet is in perpetual motion, staffers racing through the halls, shouting at each other along the way. Richard Nixon's West Wing is different, at least on the first floor: Oval Office, Cabinet Room, Roosevelt Room, President's Study, rooms for his personal secretaries, chief of staff, chief of staff's staff. Very quiet, almost without sound, as if the director, Bob Haldeman, is holding up a sign on set: "Shush, the President is working."

But a floor below, in the basement, where the two Harvard professors work, the tone is more like the West Wing as it appears on TV.

We always enter the basement from West Executive, the private street that runs between the White House and the Executive Office Building. It is also the entrance favored by those visitors who wish to avoid reporters upstairs. On the right is the Situation Room, which contains Henry Kissinger's office; beyond is the White House Staff Mess. There is a guard's desk outside the Situation Room, a couch in the corridor faces the guard, there is the men's room, and just beyond is an airless room used as a barber shop. Pat Moynihan's space is back on the left, past the elevator.

The couch is sometimes filled with celebrities, often of the Hollywood variety, who love to find an excuse to drop in at the White House. Usually social. Though some wish to be helpful. I had one TV star who wanted to put his good cause on a postage stamp. (A photograph of Richard Nixon with Elvis Presley, who will visit the president on December 21, 1970, is said to be the most requested in the National Archives.) The people on our West Wing basement couch are usually waiting to see Kissinger. We ogle them as we pass. Once I gather enough nerve to introduce myself: "Mr. Douglas, Dr. Kissinger is often very late. Perhaps you would like to have a cup of coffee in my office while waiting?" I duck my head into Pat's office to say, "Come next door, I've got Kirk Douglas here!" The three of us have twenty spirited minutes together talking movies, not politics.

When Kissinger and I happen to arrive at the same time, we follow a mock ritual: "Good morning, Henry, when are you going to end the war so that we can have money to solve our urban problems?" "Good morning, Steve, I would appreciate a distracting urban riot to give me space to end the war." (After four-plus decades the words are approximate, but the meaning accurately reflects the state of the presidency.)

A year before this I had debated Kissinger in front of a large assembly of high school students in Boston. I took Nixon's side, with Kissinger standing in for Rockefeller. We made the standard arguments, but what I most recall is how ill at ease Kissinger appeared to be. I suspected—almost certainly correctly—that he didn't spend much time talking to sixteen-year-olds. But now, as we stand side-by-side at the urinals in the West Wing basement, he tilts his head toward me and says: "Steve, you were right. This is the right man for this moment in history."

When I bump into my counterpart at the National Security Council, Colonel Alexander Haig, we always say we have to get together, but we never do. Only once am I in the Situation Room during my year in the basement, and I am surprised that it looks like any other government office. Where's the Dr. Strangelove stuff with lights flashing? My meeting in the Situation Room deals with drugs—a subject of international concern, but also a domestic issue. Nixon is to give a speech on Vietnam that evening, and when Kissinger leaves the conference table, he says, "Excuse me, gentlemen, I must translate the President's text from the original German." (This is Henry's laugh line because he is exaggerating his accent.)

Being of a rank to eat in the Staff Mess is a privilege. The room is attractive, the service efficient in the Navy style, the food is good enough and inexpensive. At 1969 prices, a three-course meal—jellied madrilène or Louisiana black bean soup, double French lamb chop, with stuffed baked potato, buttered spinach, tossed garden salad, and nesselrode nut pie or hot fudge sundae for dessert—cost $1.75. Sandwiches are 75 cents. The custom is not to invite guests who might overhear conversations that should not be public knowledge. In other words, no journalists.

People rarely turn down an invitation to dine at the White House, and Pat knows how to use this to advantage. One such lunch with Ted Hesburgh, the president of Notre Dame, is a case in point. Father Hesburgh is a member of the U.S. Civil Rights Commission, and we want to convince him to assume the chairmanship. He wants Pat to be his commencement speaker in June. This ends as a win-win—although Hesburgh, as usual, gets more than he gives. Lunch with Kingman Brewster, the president of

Yale, ends when he is handed a message that students have just occupied a building on campus. At another lunch, we introduce Ralph Nader to Nixon's consumer affairs adviser, Virginia Knauer, and her deputy, Liddy Hanford (who will become better known later as Elizabeth Dole). When Haldeman plans a second dining room for the most senior staff, he sends Mrs. Nixon's New York decorators to show Pat "their color schemes." Pat reports back to the chief of staff, "I told them as nicely but as firmly as I could that this was to be a naval officers' mess. It was not to be Schrafft's-in-the-Basement."

For our share of the basement, Pat commandeers two large rooms with windows looking out on Jackson Place. We each have a long narrow outer office in which Pat shoehorns three secretaries, and I have two secretaries and a researcher, Dick Blumenthal. Pat believes in the principle of propinquity (that is, nearness to he who is president). For us to have this space in the White House proper, the rest of Pat's staff will have to be put in the Executive Office Building. He concludes that his young assistants can cut across West Executive Street when he needs them. The EOB was built in the late nineteenth century for the departments of State, War, and Navy. It is not the preferred location in the White House complex, but for some it can be an elegant Siberia. Arthur Burns and his staff are in the EOB.

One of the nicest perks that comes with a White House office is that, if requested, the National Gallery will provide art for your walls. Pat hangs a massive self-portrait of Thomas Nast behind his desk. Since I had written a history of American political cartoons, I assume Pat is honoring the great Nast campaign against Tammany Hall corruption. But Pat's choice is neither political nor symbolic, as Pat writes Nast's grandson, who has seen a photograph of Pat's office: "It belongs to the Smithsonian and had been hanging on the wall of one of the curators who happened to be changing jobs and offices, so that it was temporarily free and I grabbed it." According to Thomas Nast St. Hill, the portrait "reflects my grandfather's despair after having lost what remained of his fortune in Wall Street."

For my office walls I borrow paintings by African American artists: a small Jacob Lawrence in the outer office and a large canvas by the wonderful Washington colorist Alma Thomas in my own office. (Forty years later, First Lady Michelle Obama will pick two paintings by Thomas to hang in the White House.)

With Liz home in Cambridge, Pat works long into the night. He shuns the cocktail party circuit and even tries to avoid formal dinners, when possible. Days often start early with staff meetings. *Time* describes him as padding "around his basement office in stocking feet like a kind of White House Superelf." For the first month, Pat arranges for daily briefings on the subjects that will be in our portfolio. Our guide is young Bureau of the Budget examiner Paul O'Neill, a future secretary of the treasury. Pat's excitement infects us, and while not all his tales are memorable, they usually have something to do with the subject at hand. On one occasion, discussing youth, Pat recalls being "in a taxi going to Brooklyn. The cabbie looks down at a *Daily News* headline on the seat. 'Look at tat. Yute rape, yute murder, yute robbery. When my kid grows up he ain't going to be no yute.'"

The bulk of Pat's days are filled with meetings, often with the president—usually as part of a group, though sometimes alone. Pat tells John Osborne of the *New Republic*, "The poor fellow is seldom more than three hours away from another meeting with me." The actual computation, taken from the president's daily diary, for January through August 1969, is that Pat spends 4,573 minutes with Nixon. (Kissinger's total is 6,955, but that doesn't include when Henry and the president are traveling abroad.)

By late afternoon we try to put aside an hour for Pat to meet with reporters or someone else who we think needs his attention. When two future British prime ministers have business in the White House, they come by to see Pat. Ted Heath and Jim Callaghan each have an aide with them, so I join the group. With Heath, it is impossible to start a lively conversation, a condition I've never before seen when Pat's in the room. But with Callaghan, themes from his and Pat's mutual Irish ancestry delight them and their assistants.

Among journalists, Pat has old friends in the Washington press corps from his days in the Kennedy and Johnson administrations—Al Otten of the *Wall Street Journal,* Mary McGrory of the *Washington Star,* David Broder of the *Washington Post.* But the *New York Times* hovers over everything in Pat's world. "[Tom] Wicker is worth reading," Pat tells Ehrlichman. "He can grasp the notion that we are doing something new." The one who must be cultivated most is James "Scotty" Reston, never far removed from another flattering note from Pat. "Dear Scotty: That was a splendid column. If only some of my colleagues up there [at Harvard] had half your balls." TV journalism rarely enters into Pat's calculations of what is important, other than the networks' Sunday morning interview shows and William Buckley on PBS.

Pat still has a massive amount of correspondence to attend to. In his correspondence, as in person, Pat can be funny, angry, kind, curt, philosophical, commonsensical. Accepting congratulations on his appointment from his accountant, he replies, "Dear Pete: You are very kind, but your real job is to keep me out of jail for income tax invasion." To "a disabled girl who collects philosophies of life from notable persons," Pat sends a quotation from the French author Georges Bernanos: "The worst, the most corrupting of lies are problems poorly stated." When his friend Irving Kristol wants a letter of recommendation for his son William, who will one day become the editor of the *Weekly Standard* and a political pundit but who first must apply to Harvard, Pat writes to the director of admissions: "Dear Chase: Billy thinks of things that don't occur to other people." In answer to a rude letter from a Cornell professor who has questioned Pat's use of Latin from the Catholic Mass: "I would have thought that any person familiar with the tenets of the Christian religion would have relatively little difficulty locating the meaning. . . . Incidentally, in your transcription, you misspelled 'peccata.'"

Most evenings, as colleagues begin to drift out of the West Wing for home, Pat goes for a swim in the indoor pool that had been built for Franklin Roosevelt (and that Nixon will soon cover over to make additional room for the press corps). Pat and Herb Klein, the communications director, are the only regular swimmers. (I went once just to claim the experience.) On the way back from a swim in August, Pat passes the Oval Office, door open while Nixon is in San Clemente. "Get up here fast!" Pat shouts into the phone. He wants me to witness how a fashionable New York decorator has desecrated this sacred room. She has bathed it in gold so bright that my young son will complain it hurts his eyes. And everywhere you look there is the Seal of the Presidency— floor, ceiling, seat cushions. "Get me Mr. Haldeman, please."

"Bob," he says when Haldeman is on the line, "I'm outside the Oval Office. Unless you do something quickly, every fucking congressman will be farting on the Seal of the Presidency." The cushions are promptly replaced.

Late in the evening, Pat is apt to have dinner in a restaurant with a friend. If Nate Owings, the chairman of the Pennsylvania Avenue Commission, is in town from San Francisco, they dine lavishly at Sans Souci. Otherwise, it's more downscale—possibly with Len Garment, whose family also doesn't live in Washington.

Pat never seems to need much sleep.

THE URBAN AFFAIRS COUNCIL

On January 23, the president's first Thursday in office, I enter the Cabinet Room at 9:30 a.m., a half hour before he is to sign Executive Order No. 11452. With a few pen strokes, Nixon will create the Council for Urban Affairs. On the table in front of where he will sit is a box of Pentel felt-tipped pens. Presidents do not sign historic documents with Pentel felt-tipped pens. We search the innards of the White House for pens that use ink and look presidential. The president must spell R-I-C-H-A-R-D N-I-X-O-N, one letter at a time, handing off pens to important people as souvenirs. But as the clock ticks down to 10 a.m., the pens we find say "LYNDON BAINES JOHNSON." Finally some "previously used" pens turn up that are simply marked "THE WHITE HOUSE." The president starts signing, the pens start leaking; by the time he reaches the final N his hands are covered with ink. Then, as if part of a prearranged Dick-and-Pat show, Moynihan whips out his Irish linen pocket handkerchief and hands it to the president, who wipes his hands—and keeps the handkerchief. Pat loses an excellent handkerchief; but it is clear our little staff is going to have to shape up.

The president tells his gathered cabinet secretaries, "Having a policy in urban affairs is no more a guarantor of success than having one in foreign affairs. But it is a precondition of success. With the creation of the Urban Affairs Council we begin to establish that precondition: The formulation and implementation of a national urban policy." The UAC will be chaired by the president and composed of the vice president; attorney general (AG); and secretaries of Agriculture; Commerce; Labor; Health, Education, and Welfare (HEW); Housing and Urban Development (HUD); and Transportation. Later the secretary of the Interior and the director of the Office of Economic Opportunity (OEO) will be added.

Ray Price, the speechwriter assigned to UAC messages, writes shortly after the first meeting, "The remarkable thing about the council is not that it has now been created but that it had not been created before. . . . The most fundamental fact about our complex of urban problems is that they are interdisciplinary and interdepartmental in nature." Yet the reason why no president has proposed a domestic advisory group comparable to the National Security Council is, possibly, that it is not a workable idea. The usual comparison to the NSC is flimsy. The players in national security are few, basically just State and Defense at the Cabinet level. They know how they fit together and where there are rubs. They are not fighting over money. The key people usually know each other from social clubs, commissions, previous service at lower levels, and by their views expressed in specialized journals and newspaper op-ed pages.

Of course, none of this holds for the domestic players. They are numerous. Their agencies can have conflicting purposes and are always in competition for limited resources. Some are elected politicians, governors, or members of Congress; others are professors or university administrators, business executives, lawyers, union leaders, group representatives. They are loosely connected, at best.

Still, if the UAC is to be productive, as Pat and Nixon will have to find out, the odds are most favorable for success at the beginning of a presidency when there is excitement, the greatest sense that cabinet officers are on the same team, and they have not yet been captured by their bureaucracies. Some of them soon will not think well of each other, but most likely not yet.

If Nixon's primary reason for creating the UAC is that it is a condition of having Pat, the arrangement still fits comfortably with his notion of how he wants to run his government. As he said in the campaign, "The job of the Presidency has gotten so big that we no longer can afford to have the President making so many of his decisions himself. . . . [H]e must have strong men as Secretary of State, Secretary of the Treasury, Secretary of Defense, who on their own as members of the team will be able to provide the leadership that the nation needs."

Nixon had spent eight years watching how Eisenhower relied on strong men: John Foster Dulles at State, George Humphrey at Treasury, Attorney General Herbert Brownell, James Mitchell when he settled in at Labor, and especially Ezra Taft Benson, who guided an unpopular agriculture policy that farmers always blamed on Benson, never Eisenhower. Perhaps Pat too, having served as an assistant secretary to Arthur Goldberg and Willard Wirtz in the Kennedy administration, starts with similarly optimistic memories of cabinets.

Unlike most presidents-elect, Nixon announced his entire cabinet all at once, on December 11. This was a clever way of closing down the idle and sometimes hurtful speculation that is a hallmark of transitions as reporters embroider the president-elect's options while waiting impatiently for the next announcement.

Instead, Nixon staged a network TV extravaganza: The future cabinet members sat in two rows facing the camera, while Nixon stood at a microphone introducing each of his twelve "new men with new ideas."

"These are strong men, they're compassionate men, they're good men," Nixon told the nation. He doesn't want "yes-men." Rather, his men are of an "extra dimension." Surveying the Washington political community, *New York Times* reporter Neil Sheehan concludes that Nixon's cabinet is viewed as "competent, dependable, pragmatic . . . dull rather than imaginative." He quotes one anonymous official who calls it "a non-Euclidian Cabinet of extra dimensions—square and flat."

The domestic part of the cabinet consists of three governors (George Romney of Michigan at HUD; John Volpe of Massachusetts at Transportation; and Alaska's Walter Hickel at Interior), a lieutenant governor (Robert Finch of California at HEW), two university administrators (Clifford Hardin, the former chancellor of the University of Nebraska, at Agriculture; George Shultz, a dean at the University of Chicago, at Labor), Nixon's campaign manager (John Mitchell as attorney general) and campaign finance chairman (Maurice Stans at Commerce).

Running the UAC means that Pat sets the agenda. He proposes; Arthur Burns reacts. Burns sees the hazards. At the first UAC meeting, on January 23, Burns tries to play the game of "cabinet covers staff," and fails. According to the minutes, "Dr. Burns and the Vice President asked if Dr. Moynihan could prepare some outline of a national urban policy, and the President agreed. Dr. Moynihan said that 'I would be glad to undertake such a task, on the condition that—and I realize that one does not ordinarily impose conditions on the President of the United States—on the condition that no one take it seriously.' Everyone roared, including the President, who first blinked, and then joined in the laughter." Point one to Dr. Moynihan.

The UAC's work will be done in committees, meaning that Pat has the authority to reward cabinet officers with committee chairmanships. This will be key to their putting before the president the matters they care about but are otherwise unlikely to get into the Oval Office. Additionally, the departments will provide experts to do the research that is beyond the reach of Pat's small staff. The system assures Pat of three cracks at the president per week—setting the UAC agenda, the council meeting, and the post-meeting debriefing.

But all this can happen only if the president comes to the meetings. As John Price, who schedules the UAC meetings, says, "Cabinet secretaries are heliotropic." The president is their sun. If he stops coming to the meetings, secretaries will send deputy secretaries. Nixon, as is well known, hates meetings. (Eisenhower had loved meetings. Nixon thought Eisenhower's cabinet meetings were "unnecessary and boring.") What Nixon loves is being alone, outlining thoughts on yellow legal pads, plotting one-on-one with Kissinger or Haldeman.

Yet Nixon keeps coming, partly because Pat raises agenda making to an art form. As much as possible, he chooses topics with some bite, adds an occasional guest speaker (Nelson Rockefeller or John Gardner, the former HEW secretary), and always stands ready with an outrageous quip. Once, when Nixon asked Pat how many women were on his staff, Pat replied, "Mr. President, I am forbidden by the Civil Rights Act of 1964 to inquire whether the members of my staff are male or female." The president stays to chair 21 of 23 meetings.

At one meeting, Pat stages a debate over where to locate a building to be constructed in Fresno, California. This is the sort of issue that presidents are not bothered with. But Pat sees an intellectual puzzle that will intrigue Nixon. The building is to be used by the Internal Revenue Service to process tax returns. The IRS wants it to be in a "good" neighborhood because during tax-collection time a lot of temporary workers are needed—mostly housewives and students. According to the IRS's brief, the agency "can effectively utilize this labor pool only if employees encounter little or no travel problems and find favorable environmental conditions." In short, put the building where it can best help the agency accomplish its mission. The General Services Administration, the agency that manages the government's real estate, proposes another site. The GSA wants to put the building in a "bad" neighborhood so that the construction will contribute to Fresno's urban renewal and, according to the GSA's brief, help "efforts directed toward the reduction in the number of our citizens who are unemployed or tied to public welfare." The IRS director debates the GSA director. The president is delighted.

(Years later, I asked Pat, "Who won?" He replied, "The IRS Service Center is on a site in a relatively nice, middle-income neighborhood, but is surrounded by poorer neighborhoods that are heavily black, Hispanic, and Asian.")

At another UAC meeting, Pat's staff detail "the demography of American youth" and "the patterns of youth unrest." Instead of the often heard anecdotes and speculations, they chart the institutional characteristics of major campus protests: 6.2 percent of colleges and universities have experienced at least one incident of "violent" protest during the academic year; 22.4 percent have experienced a "disruptive" protest; protests are twice as likely to occur at private institutions as at public institutions and three to four times more likely in nonsectarian institutions than in church-affiliated schools; they are least likely to occur at two-year colleges; and so forth. It is an electric presentation by young people not used to performing before a president. Checker Finn directs two interns—Frank Raines, 20, a student at Harvard, and Marty Fischbein, 20, a student at Antioch—who conduct the research and compile the data. (Raines will one day be the U.S. budget director and president of Fannie Mae; Fischbein and his girlfriend, TV news anchor Jessica Savitch, will die tragically in a freak car accident.)

UAC's success will also depend on the care and feeding of the members. John Price handles details with elegant precision. Like Orwell's animals, each cabinet secretary is equal, but some are more equal than others. Most equal is Attorney General John Mitchell, once Nixon's law partner and campaign manager. The first adjective Nixon puts before Mitchell's name is "tough." Pat initially wants to honor the attorney general by creating a UAC committee on crime with Mitchell as chairman. Mitchell vetoes the honor. He has no interest in inviting other department chiefs onto his turf, nor does he need the UAC to reach the president.

The potential for Pat and Mitchell to clash—and clash hard—comes in the administration's first week when Nixon reads a local newspaper editorial on crime in Washington and writes in the margin that he wants a crime statement *now*. This is clearly a call for a tough response from his Justice Department. But the District of Columbia—Washington, D.C.—is also a small piece of Pat's urban affairs portfolio. The city's population is about 70 percent black—not Nixon's constituency—yet under law the president appoints the mayor and city council. Pat's delicate task will include advising on a raft of local issues, such as whether the city should buy the privately owned D.C. Transit Company, which runs the bus system. Unexpectedly, here is an opportunity for Pat to promote a set of liberal proposals for Washington—Home Rule, a constitutional amendment to give residents a representative in Congress, and (until the amendment's passage) a nonvoting delegate in the House. Mitchell is promoting his proposals, including a "significant" increase in the role of the Bureau of Narcotics and Dangerous Drugs. Pat and Mitchell plead their cases before the president.

"Of course I'm for Home Rule. I've been for Home Rule for 22 years," says the president.

"Perhaps you should check with Congress."

"I know what Congress thinks. It's against. Why should I waste 48 hours to find out what I already know and then make them mad when I don't listen to their advice?"

In the end, the president gives his attorney general and his White House adviser most of what they want. But as Pat's bench coach, I advise him to avoid Mitchell as much as possible.

STATEMENT OUTLINING ACTIONS AND RECOMMENDATIONS FOR THE DISTRICT OF COLUMBIA, JANUARY 31, 1969
For more than 20 years I have supported home rule for the District of Columbia. I continue to support home rule. For the present, I will seek within the present system to strengthen the role of the local government in the solution of local problems. Beyond this, I will press for congressional representation for the District. In accordance both with my own conviction and with the platform pledge of my party, I will support a constitutional amendment to give the 850,000 people of the District at last a voting representative in Congress."

The problem that Commerce Secretary Maurice Stans brings to the UAC is the Department of Commerce itself. Commerce is a bunch of large pieces of government machinery thrown together—the Maritime Administration, the Bureau of the Census, the National Bureau of Standards, the Patent Office. There's no sparkle—and

Stans wants sparkle. Pat sets up a UAC Committee on Minority Business, with Stans as chairman.

Statement about a National Program for Minority Business Enterprise, March 5, 1969

As recommended by the Urban Affairs Council, I intend to establish within the Department of Commerce an Office of Minority Business Enterprise. Under the leadership of Secretary of Commerce Stans, this new office will be the focal point of the administration's efforts to assist the establishment of new minority enterprises and expansion of existing ones.

Arthur Burns writes in his diary, "Curious & interesting to see Stans trying to find something to do." Importantly, the new office doesn't cost any new money.

At the other extreme, Agriculture Secretary Clifford Hardin wants a program that will cost a great deal of money—in excess of $1 billion a year—for food stamps. Burns thinks this is "simply a scheme for redistribution of income, although not an efficient redistribution scheme." Hardin says there is hunger in America. Burns says prove it: "Insufficient caloric intake [is] something quite different from malnutrition." Haldeman writes in his diary, "Huge Burns flap because he didn't get in to see President about two sentences in 'hunger message.' Ehrlichman kept him out so he came to me and then wrote long memo to P. Feels if he can't get in when he wants to he'll have to quit."

The president turns to Pat, who writes, "There is strong evidence that very severe malnutrition, as seen in the developing countries, may lead to mental retardation. Whether less severe malnutrition as seen in the American population can affect intellectual development is just not settled. There is no good evidence to substantiate or refute." The memo is leaked, seemingly from the left, and columnists Rowland Evans and Robert Novak use this paragraph as evidence that Pat is against food stamps. But Pat's memo continues: "On the other hand, clearly, malnutrition can affect personal development in endless ways other than in the formation or destruction of brain cells. A sickly child obviously is not likely to learn as well as a healthy one. The issue is not brain damage, but rather the impairment of normal physical functioning."

SPECIAL MESSAGE TO THE CONGRESS RECOMMENDING A PROGRAM TO
END HUNGER IN AMERICA, MAY 6, 1969
The Council for Urban Affairs has for the past three months been
studying the problem of malnutrition in America. . . . That hunger
and malnutrition should persist in a land such as ours is embarrassing and intolerable. . . . I shall in a short period of time submit to
the Congress legislation which will revise the Food Stamp program
to provide poor families enough food stamps to purchase a nutri-
tionally complete diet.

Burns has argued that the budget will simply not accommodate the hunger program. To placate him, Nixon agrees to add language that "it will not be possible for the revised program to go into effect until sometime after the beginning of the calendar year 1970, that is to say after the necessary legislative approval and administrative arrangements have been made."

PAT WANTS JURISDICTION to help the exodus of Native Americans from reservations to the cities. Since the Bureau of Indian Affairs is in the Interior Department, he asks the president to put Interior Secretary Walter "Wally" Hickel on the UAC. Nixon tries to ignore the request. On Pat's third request, the president finally checks "agree." Pat and I go over to Foggy Bottom to welcome the new member. Hickel's office is huge. The president's Oval Office could fit in a corner of it. We cross the wide expanse to his desk.

"Mr. Secretary, we are here to invite you to chair the Committee on the Urban Indian."

Hickel's right arm shoots up, a forceful gesture, fingers extended. "No! I have not yet received the answer on the Indians." His hand goes up again. "I know the answer for water."

After a few "thank yous," we are dismissed and back out. On the sidewalk we double over laughing. Does this man have visions?

Meeting by meeting, the president's cabinet is getting on his nerves. After three months and three days in office, Nixon orders his chief of staff to "keep them away from him," Haldeman writes in his diary. "P said he can see why all presidents want to be left alone."

The three former governors—Romney, Volpe, and Hickel—never shut up. At one cabinet meeting Volpe asks if it's all right for a cabinet officer to say "no comment," to which the president instantly replies, "It's about time." But the prime offender is Romney. Pat reports to Nixon, "Things tend to be a one-way street with him . . . nor is HUD that responsive to White House interests." But Interior Secretary Hickel will be first to be fired. When a reporter asks why, the president answers, "I lost confidence in him and perhaps he lost confidence in me." The one for whom the president truly cares, Bob Finch, is overwhelmed at HEW, and will be quietly moved out of harm's way to the White House staff. Nixon is also looking for lesser jobs for Treasury Secretary David Kennedy (who will stay at Treasury until early 1971 when he becomes an ambassador-at-large) and Budget Director Robert Mayo (who will be named president of the Federal Reserve Bank of Chicago in June 1970).

George Shultz is the big surprise. On December 11, Nixon didn't know how to spell Shultz's name. Now, in cabinet meetings the former business school dean moves from being very quiet to being quietly very smart. As secretary of labor in a Republican administration, Shultz is underemployed, and soon the president is giving him assignments outside of his department's jurisdiction. By January 1973, the start of Nixon's second term, all of the original UAC members are gone except for Shultz, who first will be made budget director and later elevated to treasury secretary.

BEYOND THE GREAT SOCIETY

When Richard Nixon accepted the presidential nomination at the Republican National Convention in Miami Beach, he told the cheering delegates, "For the past five years we have been deluged by government programs for the unemployed, programs for the cities, programs for the poor. And we have reaped from these programs an ugly harvest of frustration, violence, and failure across the land." It is time, he promised, "to quit pouring billions of dollars into programs that have failed in the United States."

If elected, presumably this means that the days are numbered for the Office of Economic Opportunity (OEO), the nerve center of President Lyndon Johnson's Great Society. The OEO, which is based in the Executive Office of the President, administers the Community Action Program, Head Start, Job Corps, Volunteers in Service to America (VISTA), and a collection of other programs in areas such as neighborhood centers for health and drug treatment and legal services for the poor.

Where does Pat stand on the fate of these programs he had helped create? Is he a turncoat, a traitor, or a wandering intellectual raising serious questions about government urban strategy? At least some of the answers will be contained in a book Pat had written in 1968—before his appointment—and which is scheduled to be published in January. He writes to Nixon on January 24 to warn him of the coming controversy:

> At the time we discussed my joining your staff, I mentioned that I had a book coming out in January. You groaned ever so slightly!
>
> The book is entitled Maximum Feasible Misunderstanding, being an account of how the "maximum feasible participation" clause of the Economic Opportunity Act came to be. In essence the book is an enquiry into how a social science idea made its way into public policy. It is critical of the social scientists involved. Unfortunately, it is being depicted as an attack on the war on poverty itself.
>
> If you should be asked, I suggest you simply state that the book is a discussion of the role of social science in social policy, written by a professor for other professors, and in no way reflects the position of your administration on anything. Anyway, here is a copy for the White House library.

Haldeman conveys a polite "thank you" from Nixon and reports that the president "said that the book sounds particularly intriguing and that he thinks he will have to read it."

The little book—at just over 200 pages—would not be so widely noticed were Pat not now in the Nixon White House, nor would it be so harshly treated. The hostile tone is first struck in a front page review in the *New York Times Book Review* on February 3. Democratic operative Adam Walinsky opens his review with 200 words on what the book should have been about and isn't. It ends, pages later, by proclaiming that "Mr. Moynihan's appointment is evidence that in some high places, snake oil still passes for medicine." The scholar Jon Van Til of Swarthmore College concludes his review in *Social Forces* by lamenting that "what is sobering is, that of the social science fraternity, [Pat] has had more of the Presidential ear at his disposal than any of the rest of us over the past decade."

In his column in the *New Republic,* John Osborne sees within Pat's book the essence of the coming debate between Moynihan and Burns on domestic policy. Pat may tell the president that his book is a modest disagreement with some social scientists, but Osborne explains that Pat's basic argument is "what the poor need most is money, not social theories." It is a position that makes Pat an intellectual pariah in some quarters. As Osborne notes, "Mr. Moynihan could recite 'Mary had a little lamb' in Central Park and would probably be charged by somebody with inciting a riot."

The moment of truth for the OEO comes in early February when the president must decide whether to ask Congress for money to keep programs running after June 30. Nixon still wishes "to get rid of the costly failures of the Great Society . . . immediately." But as he recounts in his memoirs, there is Pat "in several long sessions in the Oval Office, [pacing] back and forth in front of my desk, waving his arms to punctuate his argument. 'All the Great Society activist constituencies are lying out there in wait, poised to get you if you try to come after them, the professional welfarists, the urban planners, the day-carers, the social workers, the public housers. Frankly, I'm terrified at the thought of cutting back too fast. Just take Model Cities. The urban ghettos will go up in flames if you cut it out.'"

Arthur Burns is not happy. He writes in his diary that "Moynihan seems to think that whatever displeases liberals is a disaster."

Pat also will explain this moment (without the arm waving) in his book *The Politics of a Guaranteed Income* (Random House, 1973):

The argument for continuity was basically prudential. The nation was shaken: possibly approaching instability; simultaneously immobilized and yet coming apart. Domestic violence had been rising on a straight trajectory and none could say it would not continue so. The domestic programs of the Kennedy and Johnson era had not prevented such deterioration, may even somehow have contributed to it, but they had achieved great visibility and great symbolic meaning as promises that somehow things would be better, or, at least, as testimonials that somebody cared. Some such programs were near to quixotic, as for example Model Cities, but these tended to be the ones most believed, and more importantly the ones that had come to involve the greatest number of people in devising dreams of a better tomorrow. To kill such programs would have been to kill the dream, and there had been enough killing. Nixon decided to carry on.

Model Cities—formally the Demonstration Cities and Metropolitan Development Act of 1966—is HUD's piece of the Great Society, a program intended to improve the coordination of existing urban renewal and rebuilding programs with a heavy emphasis on "citizen participation." In an April 7 memo written for the record, Nixon tells Pat that he is worried Secretary Romney can't handle something "as vague as" Model Cities. He directs Pat to instruct Budget Director Mayo to "strangle" Model Cities. Pat counters that perhaps Mayo should be told to squeeze Model Cities, not strangle it. Nixon replies: "We should squeeze it until it strangles."

The Great Society's "war on poverty" will thus be saved, but it will be somewhat rearranged and slightly less expensive.

SPECIAL MESSAGE TO THE CONGRESS ON THE NATION'S ANTI-POVERTY PROGRAMS, FEBRUARY 19, 1969

At my direction, the Urban Affairs Council has been conducting an intensive study of the nation's anti-poverty programs, of the way the anti-poverty effort is organized and administered, and of ways in which it might be made more effective. . . . That study is continuing. However, I can now announce a number of steps I intend to take. . . . The present authorization for appropriations for the Office of Economic Opportunity runs only until June 30, 1969. I will ask Congress that this authorization for appropriations be extended for another year.

The president also announces he intends to move Head Start and the Job Corps from OEO to the Department of Health, Education, and Welfare and the Department of Labor, respectively. (Meanwhile, Labor Secretary Shultz begins looking for a new name for the Job Corps to signal that change is coming.)

"We have salvaged the concepts and maintained the options," Pat explains to a *Wall Street Journal* reporter. Yet how can Pat, an advocate of an *income* strategy ("what the poor need most is money"), at the same time fight fiercely to keep LBJ's *service* strategy of middle-class professionals providing legal services that may or may not improve the conditions of the poor? The answer lies in urbanologist George Sternlieb's recognition of "the salutary placebo-effects of social programs." That is, symbolic rewards may be as necessary as substantive ones.

That Pat in one month wins such a major victory may be a credit to his argument, but also to the awkward position of being the resident Democrat in the Republican White House. As I write in my notes at the time, "The President does not yet take him for granted. This, in a strange way, is a plus since the President may bend over backwards to keep him relatively happy."

Nixon's potential cause for concern is stated boldly by Mary McGrory in her January 27 column in the *Washington Star:* "The skeptics still have great trouble believing that Nixon will make a major effort on the cities. The strongest counterargument is the appointment of Moynihan. They agree that Moynihan was a dazzling choice, but say, 'Of course, he won't last six months.' But if Moynihan leaves early, Nixon may be discredited in the cities. The black community regards the new President with apathy or suspicion. It has profound reservations about the author of the Moynihan Report. But Moynihan's presence is still the most powerful signal that Nixon means business in the cities. Besides, if Moynihan were to bow out prematurely, for lack of funds or support, he would document his disenchantment incomparably well."

Pat cannot afford to let this impression linger in the White House. He promptly writes the president:

I think you will want to read today's column by Mary McGrory. As you will see it is altogether friendly, but she does comment on what has become one of the favorite guessing games around Washington, namely how long Henry Kissinger and I will be here. As Mary suggests, the betting in my case is six months. Alas she does go on to suggest that if I were to leave I might "document" my "disenchantment."

I think I had better say two things on this subject.

First, I have no intention of leaving until my two years are up. Mind, the black extremists could eventually raise such a ruckus that I would be of no value to you and would have to leave, but that would be your decision. It will of course be easier if I could get, as

Martin Luther King used to say, 'a few victories.' But easy or hard, I mean to stay.

Second, regardless of what happens I wish to offer my solemn commitment that I will not in any circumstances write anything political about my experiences in the White House.

Nixon writes back: "Mary wants us to worry about what she writes—it just gives me a laugh!"

Now that OEO's future is ensured in some form, a serious problem at the White House is who will accept the unsteady assignment of being its director? Pat has a candidate. He writes to the president about a conversation he had the previous evening with Leonard Garment "discussing various possibilities. I of a sudden asked: 'Why don't you take it?' He replies, 'You know, it would be the one thing that would interest me.' I think it would be a brilliant appointment. To have someone that close to you, in that job, could have enormous consequences."

The next day Nixon tells Arthur Burns "to talk to Garment and test out his suitability for head of OEO." Burns reports back after lunching with Garment, "The only doubt I have is whether Mr. Garment has the administrative experience or skill to run an agency that thus far has been peculiarly prone to waste and even thievery." Otherwise, he thinks "Garment is brilliant." Burns's preferred candidate is William Scranton, the former governor of Pennsylvania. Strangely, Nixon does not want Scranton, who he had initially asked to be his secretary of state. "This makes no sense to me," thinks Burns. (But what really irritates Burns is that he "did not like learning from Bryce [Harlow], who heard from Flanigan, who heard from Haldeman.")

There are a lot of names flying around. Peter Flanigan, the president's assistant for high level personnel, says the president wants Walter Thayer, a New York lawyer and close associate of financier John Hay Whitney. Vernon Alden, the president of Ohio University, is sounded out. I ask Senator Charles H. Percy to see if Peter G. Peterson—who had succeeded Percy as president of Bell & Howell—might be interested. (He isn't.) The president thinks Erwin Canham, editor of the *Christian Science Monitor,* should be considered. (Too old.)

The rest of the story is contained in my notes of May 5:

Indeed, the problem was so insoluble that one Saturday morning I went over to [personnel director] Harry Flemming's office at 10, determined that I wouldn't leave until he came up with a viable name. At 11, I left nameless.

I finally hit on Don Rumsfeld. I reasoned that Rumsfeld was an attractive, ambitious young congressman from Illinois without immediate prospects of getting to Senator or Governor. I called him and was surprised when he didn't say no. Rumsfeld went abroad, making it difficult to keep working on him for several weeks. Then on Sunday, March 30, Rumsfeld having returned from England the day before, Flanigan asked me to set up a meeting at Rumsfeld's house in Georgetown with myself, Flanigan, and Flemming.

At the session, Flanigan made it clear that the President wanted him very much. Flanigan: "I said to the President that Rumsfeld has a great future in Congress, [and] the President replies, 'He has a greater future in the administration.'"

I read to Rumsfeld a draft by Dick Blumenthal of how our office envisioned OEO as the experimental, innovative arm of the government. The following Saturday I received a confidential memo from Rumsfeld declining the offer: he was the wrong man, from the wealthiest congressional district in the country, Princeton, etc., and did not want the job if it was the administration's intention to dismantle OEO. But he seemed to leave the door just the slightest open if we planned to make OEO into the imaginative operation that our paper outlined. I called him twice that afternoon. The problem was that on Monday he was going to [Maryland congressman] Rog Morton's place in the Bahamas. Then I called John Ehrlichman and asked him to fly Rumsfeld to Key Biscayne, where the President was spending Easter Sunday or we would lose him for good. He went, and the President must have been convincing. As he told me from the Bahamas, the two things that had to be ironed out were his wife's agreement and salary. I replied, "Great wives respond greatly and fancy lawyers will take care of the rest." On Monday morning Ehrlichman told Pat and me, while we were in Dwight Chapin's office waiting for the Urban Affairs Council meeting to begin, that the President had offered Rummy "two places in the Cabinet, the Vice Presidency, Dr. Burns' job and yours [pointing to Pat]."

On April 21, the president nominates Representative Donald Rumsfeld as director, Office of Economic Opportunity. Rumsfeld also will be assistant to the president, have cabinet rank, and be a member of the Urban Affairs Council. At the White House ceremony, Nixon tells the guests, "I was saying to him in our meeting in the office just before coming in here, that I remember when I was his age, 36 years of age, in 1949, I made the hardest political decision of my life. That decision was to give up a safe seat in the Congress and to run for the Senate. Don Rumsfeld, today, is 'crossing the Rubicon' to an extent."

Rumsfeld brings with him two assistants, Frank Carlucci and Richard "Dick" Cheney. All three of them will eventually serve as secretary of defense, and Dick Cheney will rise even higher in the George W. Bush administration.

The president gives the Office of Economic Opportunity a two-year extension on June 2. Pat's position is strengthened by the handoff of the OEO issue to the savvy Rumsfeld, who becomes part of his "liberal bloc" for as long as he remains in the White House.

TUTORIAL

"The Boss is in love," speechwriter Bill Safire reports. Safire means "politically 'in love,' a process that happened periodically, and often in the spring" when Nixon becomes "entranced by a new face, captivated by a new subject matter." This had happened with John Mitchell in 1967. Now "Nixon was in love again, we could tell by a look at the log—there was Moynihan in there for long hours, taking Nixon to the mountaintop of social psychology and showing him vistas of Rooseveltian glories."

The president asks Pat for his favorite political biographies. "As you know, I do quite a bit of evening reading, and I want to be sure that I am reading the best!" With Checker Finn at his elbow, Pat worries the list down to a "top 10," eliminating such worthies as Erik Erikson on Gandhi, Arthur Link on Woodrow Wilson, and Catherine Drinker Bowen on Oliver Wendell Holmes.

Pat presents the following annotated list to the president:

Autobiography, John Adams (1802)
A somewhat uneven book, but to my mind the most interesting autobiography of any of your predecessors.

Abraham Lincoln, Lord Charnwood (1917)
For my money still the best volume on Lincoln.

The Education of Henry Adams, Henry Adams (1918)
I suppose this may be the great American book. Surely it is an astoundingly perceptive account of our times, written decades before they commenced.

Talleyrand, Duff Cooper (1932)
The great French diplomatist, viewed by an extraordinarily urbane and perceptive English diplomat.

Melbourne, David Cecil (1939)
I suppose this would be my favorite political biography. I gather it was John Kennedy's also.

Hitler: A Study in Tyranny, Alan Bullock (1952)
By far the best account.

The Republican Roosevelt, John Morton Blum (1961)
A brief but unusually rewarding summary of that life.

Alexander Hamilton and the Constitution, Clinton Rossiter (1964)
An account by a great conservative historian of our great conservative statesman.

Disraeli, Robert Blake (1966)
An even more distinguished counterpart of Rossiter on Hamilton.

Zapata and the Mexican Revolution, John Womack Jr. (1969)
A new book by a powerful young historian who has managed at last to bring some order out of the chaos of the Mexican Revolution.

Later, at a private dinner with his cabinet, Nixon says (according to Bill Safire's notes): "Pat Moynihan is somewhat my mentor in terms of telling me what I should read. He doesn't think I am too well educated, so as a result, a while back he sent me a group of books to read. What surprised him was that I read them. . . . You wake up late at night—1:00–2:00—and then for two or three hours you read. . . . I would urge you some time, when you wake up in the middle of the night as I do, to pick up Cecil's *Melbourne* or maybe Blake's *Disraeli* and read it. You'll find very interesting things. You think we have problems. You should read about the problems in nineteenth-century England!"

The mentor helps his student in other ways, too. About Disraeli, Pat quotes the president as saying, "You know very well, it is Tory men with Liberal principles who have enlarged democracy." This assessment is classic Moynihan. But Pat passes off the remark as Nixon's own and makes sure it is often in print. It is a generous act of credit-sharing. As he tells the president, "The point is that journalists need an explanation, a theory of what is going on in order to make sense of the swarm of events."

The *Wall Street Journal*'s Alan Otten comments in his August 20 column (which Pat sends to the president): "Sometimes a privately uttered Presidential remark is so widely retold and printed that one has to suspect it was originally voiced with a calculating eye on the broadest possible circulation. That doesn't, of course, make the remark any less revealing; perhaps, indeed, it becomes even more significant."

Still, notes Otten, "For the most part, Tory men advanced Tory ideas, while liberal principles are pushed by liberals."

Nixon's judgment on a nineteenth-century British statesman can hardly impact Main Street, or even Congress. But it makes Nixon very pleased with himself.

SOCIAL SCIENTIST AT LARGE IN THE WHITE HOUSE

Imagine that a president can wave a magic wand: I will give you anything you want as long as it doesn't cost much money or embarrass me. This is essentially what Richard Nixon does for Pat Moynihan in the spring of 1969.

"It should be becoming obvious that he, as a liberal Democrat, has been playing it very straight with the Republican President," I write in my notes on April 1. "He has refrained from speaking out in public and has never opposed publicly anything the Administration has done." This includes Nixon's decision, which Pat vigorously opposes in a private letter to the president, to deploy the Safeguard anti-ballistic missile system. Nixon had once asked, "Could we count on him to be loyal? I don't mean Republican. I mean—you know—one of us." After three months, the president has his answer.

Nixon finds Pat "refreshing and stimulating." Fun is a commodity in short supply in this White House. As Bob Haldeman writes in his diary, "Pat is great because he provides the upbeat shot in the arm that the rest of the staff lacks." Moreover, there is pleasure for Nixon finding areas of agreement with his Democratic adviser, as when Pat writes to him, "I do not know, but strongly suspect, that especially to working-class America, the misbehavior of [college] students is seen as a form of class privilege. Which it is."

What does Pat want? Presidents know that everyone wants something—a job, a better job, an invitation, an opportunity, praise. It is this part of being president that Nixon likes least. It is why he has Haldeman and Ehrlichman around to say no. But outside of the main ring where Pat and Burns struggle over basic policy, what Pat asks for is easy to give, either because Nixon sees it is in his interest—or because he doesn't much care.

ON APRIL 24, Pat writes to the president: "I do not believe this is a racist country. But it was. And there are many only half-perceived carryovers of earlier attitudes still embedded in our everyday routines. One of these is the practice of the U.S. Government to classify its citizens as 'White' or 'Nonwhite.' White is normal. Not to be white is not to be normal. This is the only possible interpretation. Once you begin to think of it, the present practice is outrageous." Pat asks Nixon to change the system, the president checks the memo's yes box and jots "good idea."

Pat then calls his office representatives from Commerce, Labor, HEW, and the Bureau of the Budget to discuss different possibilities for how to classify the population. He asks James Farmer, who is now the assistant secretary of HEW, to survey how the black community would like to be classified in government statistics. Farmer reports deep differences between the young and old over the use of black and Negro.

On August 15, the Bureau of the Budget's Office of Statistical Policy announces that the term "nonwhite" will be eliminated from use in the government's statistical publications. (The Census

Bureau will use the term "Negro" until 2013, when it is dropped in favor of "black" or "African American.")

I relate news of the change to White House spokesmen Ron Ziegler and Herb Klein: "This is the sort of thing that will be overlooked by the press. . . . This was done solely on the initiative of the President (acting on the suggestion of Dr. Moynihan). . . . This is a positive accomplishment in the field of human rights and done without fanfare."

But if the media does pay attention to the change, it escapes my notice.

PAT DOES NOT assume the traditional role of the White House intellectual-in-residence—arranging seminars for the president and keeping him informed of interesting academic research. In his mind, Pat is first and foremost a policy adviser. But there are two findings of social science to which he wants to direct the president's attention, and, by doing so, some things happen that would not otherwise have happened.

The first is Pat's awareness of the exceptional importance of the first five years of life to children's long-term health and welfare. He alerts Nixon to "new knowledge, new facts" about how early in life learning begins. "We know today—and with each day our knowledge grows more detailed—that the process of human development is in certain fundamental ways different from what it has been thought to be." This is a theme Pat often returns to. On February 19, the president tells Congress, "So crucial is the matter of early growth that we must make a national commitment to providing all American children an opportunity for healthful and stimulating development during the first five years of life." On April 9, Nixon announces the establishment of the Office of Child Development.

The second is Pat's concern over the ramifications that "the earth will contain over seven billion human beings by the end of [the twentieth] century." It is the moment when the so-called Population Bomb is gaining potency as an issue among environmentalists, and Pat, while not a leader in the environment movement, carries its message to the president. On July 18, the president sends a long and impassioned message to Congress on the "pressing problems" of the "dramatically increasing rate of population growth." Since this coincides with Apollo 11 heading for the moon, Nixon can perorate, "Let us act in such a way that those who come after us—even as they lift their eyes beyond the earth's bounds—can do so with pride in the planet on which they live." In March of the following year, the president will establish the Commission on Population Growth and the American Future, to be chaired by John D. Rockefeller III. Pat, as is his practice, makes sure Nixon sees the "highly favorable and enthusiastic" response to his population growth initiative, even in "a number of lesser-known and small town newspapers."

PAT HAS AN experience not shared with any other person in the Nixon White House: he has previously served in a federal department and knows how difficult it is to conduct business when each agency organizes the United States differently. HUD's group of states in "Region I" will not be the same states that HEW puts in its "Region I." The headquarters of the Labor Department in "Region II" will not be in the same city as the "Region II" headquarters of the Small Business Administration. For almost 20 years, presidents have paid lip service to aligning the domestic agencies and putting the same states in the same regions, with the same regional headquarters. "It is," Pat explains, "perhaps the least exciting subject in government, and that has been the source of the problem, just not in being able to muster the attention of persons to its absolutely essential nature." Pat concludes that Nixon must "take it up early and get it done fast [before] other more glamorous issues drive it into the next administration." It is on the agenda of the first UAC meeting on January 23.

On March 27, with Pat as the driving force within the White House, the president announces that five agencies—Labor, HEW, HUD, OEO, and SBA—will henceforth divide the country into eight regions, with the same states in each region and with each region having the same headquarters.

What Pat sees as a "low level of public interest" now becomes "a rather specific level of local opposition." This is illustrated by a reporter's question when the plan is announced: "I would like to talk about Kansas City. You are going to move HEW, OEO and Labor. That is 825 people involved. That is $10 million a year in payroll. HEW said it will cost them $800,000 to go to Denver. The Missouri and Kansas delegations, Republicans and Democrats alike, are upset. They don't understand why you are moving three bigger offices to Denver instead of two smaller ones to Kansas City."

Based on an "eyes only" draft memo from the Bureau of the Budget, I have to tell Pat that "our posture on Kansas City will be virtually impossible to defend in the course of cross-examinations in Congressional hearings." Moreover, Warren Magnuson, the Democratic senator from Washington and chairman of the key appropriations subcommittee, is likely to attach a rider telling the president "to go back to the drawing board and return next year with a plan which has been thought through, priced out, and purged of politics." The problem, notes Dwight Ink, the memo's author, is that "regional status for Seattle has been a goal of Senator Magnuson for years. He is very emotional on the issue."

On May 21, the president—having gone back to the drawing board—issues another statement. Forget about the March 27 announcement, he says in effect. The structure of the government now will be arranged in *ten* regions, not *eight*. Region VII will have its headquarters in Kansas City; Region VIII will be headquartered in Denver. Another region, consisting of Alaska, Idaho, Oregon, and Washington, will have its headquarters in Seattle.

Pat tells a press conference, "This is the first time in the history of the American Republic that the regional boundaries of the major domestic programs will be coterminous."

ONE OF PAT'S cherished proposals is to urge Nixon to push the country to take "the long perspective," to focus "our attention farther into the future." The vehicle he recommends is a commission on national goals. Two previous presidents—Hoover and Eisenhower—had such commissions, but both had formed them when they were nearly out the door. According to Len Garment, "Arthur Burns disliked the idea intensely." Another commission is well outside his agenda of budget tightening. As a result, Pat has to accept a compromise: the president will appoint a national goals research staff, not a national goals commission.

STATEMENT ON THE ESTABLISHMENT OF THE NATIONAL GOALS
RESEARCH STAFF, JULY 12, 1969
Only by focusing our attention farther into the future can we marshal our resources effectively in the service of those social aims to which we are committed, such as eliminating hunger, cleaning up our environment, providing maximum opportunity for human development during the critical first 5 years of life, maintaining and improving standards of education and medical care, reducing welfare dependency, and making our cities livable for all. . . . We

should expect this look into the future to be both exciting and sobering: exciting, because it will show how great is the reach of the possible; sobering, because it also will show that there are some problems against which the best will in the world can produce only painfully slow progress.

But the White House, as usual, is overwhelmed by the now. The future will have to wait. Garment—who is tapped by the president to head the effort—soon has to deal with the American Indian Movement occupying Alcatraz Island in San Francisco Bay. When the National Goals Research Staff is finally terminated in 1970, it has produced only one report, "Toward Balanced Growth: Quantity with Quality," assembled by Professor Raymond Bauer of Harvard and anticipating such emerging issues as consumerism, environmental degradation, and U.S. population shifts.

The report opens with a long essay by Pat about "the need for increasingly accurate and easy-to-follow social data that describes the past and present, and reasonably projects the future." This theme will eventually be reduced to Pat's most quoted one-liner: "You are entitled to your own opinions, but not to your own facts."

AN UNEXPECTED WAVE of the president's wand sends Pat off on an international adventure to lead the preparations for a new NATO committee. Diplomatic luncheons in London and negotiations in Brussels are catnip to someone who researched his dissertation on the International Labor Organization while a Fulbright Scholar at the London School of Economics.

The assignment has an odd history.

On Saturday, April 5, I am having breakfast in the White House Mess when Bob Ellsworth comes by my table. He is a former Kansas congressman about to be Nixon's ambassador to

NATO. Next week, he says, the president will speak at the 20th anniversary of the North Atlantic Council. "Appreciate any good ideas," he adds, dropping Ray Price's draft of the speech on the table. Returning to my office, I wonder if Nixon would consider proposing an Urban Affairs Council for NATO. I call Pat at home in Cambridge. "Yes," he says, "a good idea." I ask Pat to tell me what countries do good things that we could learn from.

Pat gives examples; I take notes and send Ellsworth my suggested language: "We in the United States have much to learn from the experiences of our NATO allies in their handling of internal matters: the care of infant children in West Germany; the 'new towns' policy of Great Britain; the development of depressed areas program in Italy; the great skill of the Dutch in dealing with high density areas; the effectiveness of urban planning by local governments in Norway, and the experiences of the French in metropolitan planning. (Tick off an example for each NATO country.)"

Kissinger endorses the idea, urging the president to underline the principle "that the security of this alliance should be broadly construed to involve not only its physical safety against external attack but the ability of our countries to cope with the problems *within* our societies."

ADDRESS AT THE COMMEMORATIVE SESSION OF THE NORTH ATLANTIC COUNCIL, APRIL 10, 1969

I strongly urge that we create a committee on the challenges of modern society. . . . We in the United States have much to learn from the experiences of our Atlantic allies in their handling of internal matters: for example, the care of infant children in West Germany, the "new towns" policy of Great Britain, the development of depressed areas programs in Italy, the great skill of the

Dutch in dealing with high density areas, the effectiveness of urban planning by local governments in Norway, the experience of the French in metropolitan planning.

Pat sets off for Brussels in September to help prepare a charter for the Committee on the Challenges of Modern Society (CCMS). However, as Pat says in a classified report to the president, he quickly finds that "no one seems to believe that our objectives are what we state them to be, namely to use the opportunity provided by the existence of NATO to move ahead on multi-national cooperation on environmental and societal matters which are serious, and which we take seriously."

The Europeans are puzzled. Is Nixon using the "environment" to offset his unpopular Vietnam policies? Is this part of Nixon's plan for East-West détente? Pat finds that "the French and Germans were extremely cautious about everything. . . . The Netherlands representative was, at times, barely civil. The Norwegians clearly had instructions to be quite negative. . . . The atmosphere was reserved and even chilled." Pat also worries that the State Department "is probably not very interested. . . . They don't especially understand it and probably don't especially approve what appears to be an unnecessary distraction from the fundamental purposes of The Alliance."

Our European allies resent being pushed around by the Americans. The State Department resents being pushed around by the White House. But CCMS continues a steady stream of pilot projects.

PAT TAKES PRIDE in telling Nixon the history of the Presidential Medal of Freedom. Once there was a rarely noticed "Medal of Freedom," established during World War II and awarded principally to spies who aided the war effort. President Eisenhower wanted to create a national honors system, but his legislation was blocked in the Senate as smacking of the "titles of nobility" that the Constitution forbids. President Kennedy also wanted to create an honors system and gave the assignment to Labor Secretary Arthur Goldberg, who passed it along to Special Assistant Moynihan, who then performed a feat of creative engineering: Knowing that no honors proposal could get through Congress, Pat simply proposed resurrecting the "Medal of Freedom," renaming it the "Presidential Medal of Freedom," and announcing it as "the nation's highest civil honor." (These changes are not enough to keep Tom Wicker of the *New York Times,* on the occasion of the inaugural awards in 1963, from observing that the award is "similar to the annual honors list of the British monarch.")

With Len Garment's help, Pat puts together a list of names to "stimulate" the president's thinking on who is medal-worthy in 1969. Among Nixon's choices are the Apollo 11 astronauts (Buzz Aldrin, Neil Armstrong, and Michael Collins), actors Gregory Peck and Bob Hope, novelist Ralph Ellison, Henry Ford II, heart surgeon Michael DeBakey, Lyndon Johnson's secretary of defense, Clark Clifford, and civil rights leader Whitney Young. Pat explains that the award can also be given "with distinction," and so a Presidential Medal of Freedom with Distinction is presented to his old boss, Averell Harriman.

But the award of greatest distinction goes to Duke Ellington, who receives his medal on April 29 at a black-tie celebration of his 70th birthday at the White House. "The Duke's Party" rates page-after-page of commentary in the May 10 issue of the *New Yorker.* The president presents the award. The Duke, "in the French style," kisses the president on both cheeks. The president blushes.

The president sits at the piano and plays "Happy Birthday" in the key of G. Everybody sings.

The band steps forward: Hank Jones, Jim Hall, Milt Hinton, Louis Bellson, Bill Berry, Clark Terry, Urbie Green, J. J. Johnson, Gerry Mulligan, and Paul Desmond. High points, according to the *New Yorker*, include "Gerry Mulligan's impassioned 'Sophisticated Lady'; a gorgeous Urbie Green solo in 'I Got It Bad and That Ain't Good'. . . exhilarating choruses of 'Perdido,' by Earl Hines; and a caroming Louis Bellson drum solo in 'Caravan.'" Ellington comes back to the platform to improvise "a slow, Debussy-like melody," which he dedicates to Mrs. Nixon.

The party moves to the East Room for dancing and a jam session. "Lou Rawls was shouting the blues, and he was followed by [Billy] Eckstine and Joe Williams. . . . Then Ellington and Willie the Lion Smith . . . played a duet, and so did the Lion and Marian McPartland." Len Garment, who is most responsible for the party, and once played saxophone in Woody Herman's band, will later write in his memoirs, *Crazy Rhythm* (1997), that he brought his clarinet to the party, "a more credible instrument to whip out casually."

The Nixons go to bed shortly after midnight. The rest of us dance and play and listen until after two. Thirty-three years later, in 2002, Blue Note Records will put out a recording of the concert from a cassette tape saved by Len Garment.

THE 75-DAY MARK: APRIL 14

On an early day in the life of the Nixon administration, speechwriter Ray Price sends the president a memo urging that he not play by "the old rules . . . of measuring progress according to the standards established by Roosevelt in his first 100 days. . . . The fact of the matter is that the nation still is suffering from the first 100 days of Johnson, from the first 100 days of Kennedy, and even, lingeringly, from the first 100 days of Roosevelt. It should be neither our plan nor our style to repeat those 100 days stunts."

It is a nice idea. But Nixon knows the press will never give a president the luxury to ignore this traditional benchmark. Rather, the problem for Nixon is that he will not have an impressive list of domestic actions to announce at the end of 100 days. *Time* writes of the administration's "leisurely pace" and accusations of a "do-little presidency." The insiders' case against Pat Moynihan and Arthur Burns will be that they distract Nixon from concentrating on vital international concerns, and create for him the sort of "people conflict" that he has never been able to handle. But more immediately, the battling professors are pushing his timetable well beyond 100 days.

Nixon tries to minimize his 100-days problem by sending Congress a "special message" after 75 days about his forthcoming proposals. John Mitchell is represented with "new measures to combat organized crime" and "a detailed plan for combating crime in the District of Columbia." Postmaster General Winton Blount gets "a comprehensive reorganization of the Post Office Department." Bud Wilkinson, the great University of Oklahoma football coach and now a White House consultant, will have a program to "enlist the great, vital voluntary sector more fully."

Arthur Burns gets promises to fight inflation, support for the monetary policies of the Federal Reserve, a cut in fiscal year 1970 expenditures by $4 billion, and "reform of the tax structure." "At the same time," the president writes, "I sent more than 100 directives to the heads of various departments and agencies, asking their carefully considered recommendations on a wide range of domestic policy issues." These are Burns's task force reports from the transition, and they range from matters of oceanography, rural development, and lumber and plywood prices to oil import quotas. These reports had been sent to the president and to the departments with Pat being out of this loop. In retrospect, Pat must be relieved to avoid reviewing issues that he would find more tedious than elevating. He is a man of eclectic interests, yet also strong disinterests. At the same time, Burns—or at least his small staff—is being spread over an exceptionally broad range of subjects.

Pat's contributions to Nixon's list of achievements as of April 14 are numerous. The president notes the creation of the Urban Affairs Council, the reorganization of the system of federal regional offices, and the ongoing overhaul of the Office of Economic Opportunity and its programs. He mentions forthcoming recommendations for home rule and congressional representation for the District of Columbia, "vigorous and innovative" programs to combat hunger and nutrition, and "an effort to increase the effectiveness of our national drive for equal employment opportunity" through the creation of a Minority Business Enterprise office in the Commerce Department. Even more notable is that the president twice stresses his administration's concern for "the child under five" and "our commitment to the first five years of life."

The Nixon record is ideologically moderate, but it is moderate by averaging—moving sharply right, followed by moving sharply left. Moving sharply right is to be expected. Nixon owes his election to a so-called Southern strategy, a "law and order" campaign with racial overtones that is promoted by South Carolina's senator Strom Thurmond and state Republican Party chairman Harry Dent. Despite the independent candidacy of former Alabama governor George Wallace, Nixon manages to carry Virginia, Tennessee, North Carolina, South Carolina, and Florida—crucial pieces in his narrow victory over Democrat Hubert Humphrey. Harry Dent is now on the White House staff as the liaison to his wing of the party.

On the left, however, Pat is owed nothing except the opportunity to make his case before the president. Burns is irritated that Pat "is blind to the importance of the President's retaining of his political power base." But Pat is having a better beginning than an outsider might expect. Some wonder if he is holding back. There are intra-administration fights in which he seems to be staying out of the crossfire.

Pat is "picking his shots carefully," conclude columnists Evans and Novak. For example, Bob Finch at HEW and John Mitchell at Justice argue over when and where to enforce Title VI of the 1964 Civil Rights Act, which authorizes cutting off funds to school districts that are not desegregating "with all deliberate speed." Finch wants to cut off funds; Mitchell does not. This is a deeply divisive issue within the Republican Party. Pat holds his fire, saving his ammunition.

Also on the horizon is the prospect of the president sending Congress a massive program to reform the welfare system. Nixon's 75-day message explains, "Our studies have demonstrated that tinkering with the present welfare system is not enough. We need a complete re-appraisal and re-direction of programs which have aggravated the troubles they were meant to cure, perpetuating a dismal cycle of dependency from one generation to the next."

This is, in other words, Pat's chance to close in on that elusive beast—his Moby Dick—that he has been pursuing since the Moynihan Report was leaked in 1965. The president offers Pat an opportunity for restitution—if not revenge—for the blows he still feels from 1965. He knows that he was right and he was wronged, and Nixon, this strange ally, has made him an Ahab in pursuit of the white whale of welfare reform.

MOYNIHAN AT NOTRE DAME: JUNE 1

Our lunch in the White House Mess on April 9 with Father Theodore Hesburgh, the president of Notre Dame, is a delight. Ted Hesburgh rates among the world's most charming men, notable, like Pat, for being quoted. ("All of us are experts at practicing virtue at a distance.") He agrees to remain on the U.S. Commission on Civil Rights for a year and to assume the chairmanship from John Hannah. The president will be indebted to him. Pat, in turn, agrees to be his commencement speaker in June.

After Pat goes off to other business, Hesburgh and I go to my office to work out a few minor details relating to the commission. He wants John Gardner to be vice chairman. We want Steve Horn, soon to be president of California State University at Long Beach. Since I am quite sure that Gardner won't accept, I only have to wait out Hesburgh, since he doesn't object to Horn. (The president appoints Horn on May 29.) We have only a few more requests, most significantly removing Staff Director Howard Glickstein, whom we see as representing the Johnson administration. We have an excellent candidate, Al Abrahams, who is the administrative assistant to liberal Republican senator Mac Mathias of Maryland.

Hesburgh readily agrees to all our requests and leaves my office to meet Abrahams. What a sweet, reasonable guy. Later in the day, he calls to say that while he likes Al very much, he feels Abrahams doesn't have a deep enough knowledge of civil rights for the job. Okay, I say. After all, rarely have I dealt with such a reasonable man. The next day—partly after talking to Abrahams—I realize I have been completely taken. Hesburgh never had any intention of accepting Abrahams, and he only went to see him in order to tell me that he wouldn't do. I write in my notes, "Remember not to play poker with the Good Father." To satisfy Hesburgh, the president must reappoint Glickstein, which he does on June 16.

On June 1, Pat goes to Notre Dame and cannot resist telling the students and their parents of "growing up in New York City in the poverty-ridden 1930s, and yet possessing in that Notre Dame football team a symbol of tribal might and valor that can stir the blood atingle to this day. O, the golden Saturday afternoons when, in the name of every Irish kid caught in the social wreckage of the Eastern slums, thunder indeed shook down from the skies, and those mighty Polish tackles swamped the Navy . . .!"

This is all the fun Pat has to offer the graduates. Otherwise, the speech is deeply philosophical about "the quest for divinity [in] a secular form" and America facing a religious—not political—crisis. There is also a great deal of directed anger at university intellectuals in this year of campus turmoil. Pat has not adjusted his opposition to the Vietnam War while in Nixon's White House, but he is increasingly troubled by faculty acquiescence to student rioting.

There are analogues, indeed precedents, for the violence of the streets, the poor, the police, and such-like. But nothing like the present patterns of threats to and actual assault on university institutions and university members has ever before occurred.

Indeed, some good could come of this if the excesses of the moment were to serve to restore some perspective on just what universities are and what they can do. They are institutions inhabited by younger and older persons often of very great abilities, but usually of very limited experience. With respect to their individual specialties, the judgment of the professors is singularly valuable. But their collective judgment is no better—could, indeed, be worse—than that of the common lot of men. This is not an incidental, random fact; it is a fundamental condition of human society, and the very basis of democratic government.

All this is to the good. What is bad is that the diffusion of violence to the intellectual life of our society is likely to lead to even greater failure to state our problems correctly than has been the case to date. This is so for the most elemental of reasons. Intellectual freedom in the American university has now been seriously diminished. It is past time for talking about what might happen; it has happened. We would do well to clear our minds of cant on that subject. Especially in the social sciences, there is today considerably less freedom than there was a decade ago; and we should expect that it will surely be ten to twenty years before what we would hope to be a normal state will be restored.

I deem it essential that this almost suddenly changed situation be more widely understood; otherwise, the sickness of the time will gradually come to be taken for a normal condition of health—and that would be a blow not merely to the age, but to the culture. But if we do perceive our circumstance for what it is, if we do come to accept that for reasons of prudence, or cowardice, or incompetence,

*or whatever, faculties have been everywhere allowing principles and
men to be sacrificed, we will at least return the understanding that
something has gone wrong, something that it may be possible someday to right.*

*It is important then to survive, with our faculties, as it were, as
little diminished as possible, and to seek to understand the times—
which is to say to state the problems of the time correctly.*

Back in Washington, Pat informs the president that the speech
will be published in September by the *American Scholar,* the organ
of the Phi Beta Kappa Society. "Good job!" writes Nixon. "It is
reassuring to have a true intellectual-in-residence!"

NIXON ALONE

Throughout 1967 and 1968, Richard Nixon explained his idea of the presidency to interviewers like Theodore H. White: "I've always thought the country could run itself domestically without a president. All you need is a competent Cabinet to run the country at home. You need a president for foreign policy."

Nixon says this because he wants it to be true, and he thinks it can be true from watching Dwight Eisenhower for eight years. But Eisenhower's experience in cabinet making is wildly exceptional in presidential history. As a five-star general who had been a popular hero in a popular war, Eisenhower could have had anyone he wanted in his cabinet. No one turned him down—a statement no other president of the modern era can make. Moreover, Ike in 1952 carried the Republican Party to victory, rather than the other way around, and as such he did not have to make the usual political adjustments when elected. Nixon, on the other hand, has scored a narrow party victory in 1968, and his cabinet includes people he needed to get there, rather than people he necessarily likes or trusts. Moreover, Eisenhower's skill at managing his cabinet had been honed by managing the Allied High Command in Europe. These are not Nixon's skills.

Then too, simply put, Nixon wants to be alone. Word goes out to the staff that Wednesdays are off-limits, reserved for thinking time. Bob Haldeman calls this the "Clear Wednesday Policy." The president moves his "working" office across the street to the Executive Office Building; the Oval Office will be for official meetings and ceremonial events. While at Duke Law School, unlike the students who formed study groups, Nixon studied his cases alone. Clues to his solitary nature are spread throughout his remarkably revealing 1962 book *Six Crises:* "The necessary soul-searching of deciding. . . . the tension which builds up in a crisis. . . . concentrating completely on how to meet the danger." A high degree of solitude seems to be necessary for Nixon, even in the White House, and this is understood by his chief of staff.

On foreign policy, as has always been his plan, Nixon turns inward to the national security adviser and his staff. With Henry Kissinger established in the Situation Room, this leaves little room for Secretary of State Bill Rogers in policymaking. Kissinger excels at flattering the president; not born to the manor, he has acquired useful courtier skills along the way. They are an unlikely pair. But their differences, Nixon concludes, help to make the partnership work. Kissinger proves to the president that he is an ideal companion with whom to be alone.

But on domestic policy Nixon is not looking for an ideal companion. He had never planned on a 50-50 split of his time as president. His overarching interest in foreign policy is consumed with pressing matters in Vietnam, the Soviet Union, China, and the Middle East. The foreign increasingly pushes out the domestic. In the 726 pages that Nixon will devote to the White House years in his 1978 memoirs, only 11 percent involve domestic policy.

Nixon may have dreamed of cabinet-centered domestic policy-making, but the cabinet-less policymaking he gets boils down to the struggle between Pat Moynihan and Arthur Burns. Policymaking is more efficient, more hidden from the nattering press, and easier for a president to control when the players are all within the White House rather than spread around Washington. The disadvantages relate to leaving out important players—in the executive agencies, in Congress, in interest groups, even in the media—who have a stake in the implementation. In their first year presidents care about producing policy; implementation comes later.

Pat proves to be an amazingly agile bureaucratic player. From the moment he chooses to put himself in small offices in the West Wing basement, while Burns chooses greater comfort across the street in the Executive Office Building, devotees of Washington politics understand who has the surer touch. Looking back from 1978, Marty Anderson, a worthy opponent, will credit Pat's "previous experience in Washington" as a reason for his being "extraordinarily effective."

Putting aside the merits of their proposals or their bureaucratic skills, when Pat is invited into Nixon's exclusionary world he charms and entertains the president. Burns, on the other hand, is too ponderous for a steady diet. At one meeting Burns wishes to add "just one word of caution," to which the president cautions, "Not too many!"

Nixon gives Burns cabinet rank, but not a key to his two-man inner circle. Pat, as the designated Democrat, understands his place. Burns finds it increasingly difficult to get past Haldeman and Ehrlichman to see the president in private. This is painful as he has had a long and useful history with Nixon that means a great deal to him. Burns pleads with Ehrlichman, who is increasingly Nixon's consigliere on domestic matters, to try to make the president understand that the welfare proposal Pat is drafting is alien to the president's philosophy. Ehrlichman replies, probably not in jest, "Don't you realize the President doesn't have a philosophy?" When Burns, leaving a meeting, suddenly remembers something he just forgot to tell Nixon, Haldeman says, "Your appointment is over, Dr. Burns. Send a memo."

Burns tries to adjust his strategy to block Pat by harkening back to when Eisenhower's cabinet was worth lobbying: he now turns to the Nixon cabinet for support.

WELFARE REFORM:
MOYNIHAN'S WHITE WHALE

One of Pat's first memos "For the President," on January 31, sets out the importance of promptly addressing the explosion in urban welfare. Using New York City as his example, he began, "Like the girl and the book about crocodiles, I fear that I may end up telling you more about welfare in New York City than you want to know. . . . Estimates are that one out of every eight New Yorkers, over one million people, will receive public assistance in 1969, at a total cost of two billion dollars."

With capitalization and underlining, Pat arrived at a "PROPOSAL FOR PRESIDENTIAL ACTION: I believe the time has come for a President to state what increasingly is understood: that welfare as we know it is a bankrupt and destructive system."

The welfare program Pat asks Nixon to end—Aid to Families with Dependent Children (AFDC)—covers 6 percent of all children under the age of 18. This includes 40 percent of all poor children in the United States, of whom two-thirds are in families headed by women. "For the most part, a poor child is not eligible for AFDC unless his father dies or deserts," reports

Robert Lampman, University of Wisconsin expert on poverty. The largest portion of AFDC families comes from divorce, desertion, or illegitimacy. In short, needy children are denied benefits not of their own doing. This is "an insane piece of social engineering" that encourages the breakup of families, concludes Yale economist James Tobin, the future Nobel laureate.

There is another aspect to thinking about welfare that Pat brings to the White House. It may eventually enter into policy. It is the theme that was deeply embedded in his controversial 1965 report, *The Negro Family*. When Pat later writes about what happened in 1969 and 1970, he will begin, "The issue of welfare is the issue of dependency. It is different from poverty. To be poor is an objective condition; to be dependent, a subjective one as well. . . . [D]ependency becomes a stigma. This is the heart of it. The issue of welfare involves a stigmatized class of persons."

The system Pat most admires is one that provides "children allowances," a non-contributory, no-means-tested plan for family welfare. But his staff man on welfare, John Price, reminds him, "Your children's allowance thing is over the moon." Price knows where the Republican Party is located. So Pat knows the problem, but he does not yet have a solution he can offer the president. Initially all Pat asks Nixon to do is call for national minimum standards for welfare and to form a national commission.

The national standards proposal comes from a transition task force on public welfare headed by Richard Nathan, a former Nelson Rockefeller campaign aide, who will be the assistant director for human resources in the Budget Bureau. The Nathan Report merely addresses the differences among the states in payment levels to poor families. The original New Deal program left AFDC benefit levels to the states to determine, and the difference between high and low states is now almost 10 to 1. The Nathan

Report describes its recommendations as "an incremental, not a radical, overhaul."

The Nathan Report goes to the Council for Urban Affairs' Welfare Subcommittee, chaired by HEW secretary Bob Finch. There it is marinated by his department's policy wonks and comes out looking like a negative income tax (NIT). In another line of work this might be called bait-and-switch. John Price shows Pat how the proposal is structured. "You've got it! That's it!" Pat exclaims—at last he has his welfare plan.

Here is how the idea came about. At HEW in 1968, the Office for Planning and Evaluation—run by Assistant Secretary Alice Rivlin and Deputy Assistant Secretary (Income Maintenance) Worth Bateman—developed an income-supplement plan for poor households headed by a working male. The plan was ultimately rejected by HEW secretary Wilbur Cohen and President Lyndon Johnson. But Rivlin and Bateman, who remained at HEW for a few carryover months in 1969, quietly passed the idea across party lines to the incoming administration. Thought Bateman, "I wasn't going to be there very long anyway. I might as well make one more attempt to put forward this negative tax program. It would be shot down, but it would have been fun anyway."

Instead, the proposal appeals to Finch and his under secretary, Jack Veneman, who had been the Republican spokesman on welfare matters in the California legislature. Veneman's deputy, Bob Patricelli, a former counsel on a Senate subcommittee, will be the point man. "Nobody in their wildest dreams ever thought that the Nixon administration would buy a program like this," remembers Bateman. "I don't think anybody could convey the surprise."

The hand-off may have been Democrat to Republican, but the idea of a negative income tax as welfare policy is actually most associated with the conservative economist Milton Friedman.

When he worked for the Treasury Department in 1943, Friedman worried about low-income workers whose incomes rose and fell from one year to the next. Why not a system where workers pay taxes to the government in good years and the government pays taxes to them in bad years? Might this even be a device for eliminating poverty? The Ripon Society's young Republicans are also intrigued by the idea.

If Pat is surprised and delighted, Burns is suspicious and furious. Burns's philosophical objection to NIT, he writes the president, is that it means government is "moving away from the concept of welfare based on disability-related deprivation and need to the concept of welfare as a matter of right." He reminds Nixon that he is on record opposing NIT. Journalist Daniel Schorr explains, "Burns stands for the conservative belief that money should not be handed out for not doing anything. He speaks for the enraged hard-working, tax-paying citizens who resent seeing others supported by the government."

Pat needs a name change—like "guaranteed income." Burns's deputy, Marty Anderson, isn't going to let him get away with this sleight-of-hand. "Let us call a spade a spade! This is a negative income tax!" A passionate, pound-the-table moment in a White House debate. Pat returns fire, "Let us remember Oscar Wilde's conclusion. Anyone who would call a spade a spade should be compelled to use one!" The cabinet secretaries laugh—as Pat means them to. But the two academics understand the seriousness of the encounter. Pat is now acting as the advocate, not the traditional role of the executive secretary of a cabinet council. Finch should be in command, but he is in the hospital, worn down by a collection of conflicts, and Pat feels he must step in.

When Nixon appointed Pat to his staff in December, the *Chicago Tribune* cautioned its readers, "It is unlikely, for example, that Nixon would ever embrace Moynihan's concepts of a family allowance for the poor." Yet Nixon keeps pressing for more and more information. Welfare is the one domestic issue that truly absorbs him. Both sides feed the president's interest. And after cabinet debate, the concept of a guaranteed income or a negative income tax is finally given what is considered a more neutral name. Pat argues, "In truth, the Family Assistance Plan (FAP) is in some ways the most significant departure yet made from the Poor Laws of Elizabethan England from which our present practices have descended with all too little change. . . . The plan is simple. Every American family with children is guaranteed a minimum income, according to the number of persons in the family. For those families with no income, this minimum guarantee is paid. But those families with income, especially the families of the working poor where an employed father struggles to maintain his wife and children on an income that is simply too little, there would also be a payment, so that total income would rise to more acceptable levels. The higher the family income, of course, the lower the Federal supplement."

Anderson wants the president to understand the consequences of the Speenhamland system, a British scheme from the late 1700s that also provided wage supplements to the poor. Anderson writes to Nixon to describe how the great economic historian Karl Polanyi concluded that Speenhamland led to "the pauperization of the masses, who almost lost their human shape in the process." The president asks Pat for his opinion of Anderson's opinion of Speenhamland. Pat responds, "It seems absurd to trouble you with controversies concerning the post-Napoleonic economic history of Britain, but if you like. . . ." Pat means to cast Anderson's concerns into the bin of historical irrelevancy. Yet he actually takes the challenge very seriously and rushes for support to two friends who are great historians, Gertrude Himmelfarb at Brooklyn College and J. H. Plumb of Christ's College, Cambridge. Speenhamland, he tells Nixon, had been no great success but no great failure either.

After an April meeting with Nixon in Key Biscayne, Burns writes in his diary that he "detects" the president is "leaning" toward the Moynihan proposal, and concludes that he must "set about developing an alternative plan for welfare reform." He asks Nathan to beef up the original task force report calling for national standards. This is what Pat had been for and Burns against in January, causing Pat to later write, "[As] the dispute moved through a series of stages, at each one the participants appeared willing to do more than they had thought necessary or sufficient in the preceding stage."

Pat, also sensing victory, understands that it is best for all if Burns has a victory too. In addition to welfare reform, an important piece of what will be in Nixon's domestic program is called revenue-sharing, a proposal to return a portion of federal tax dollars to states and other localities. While both Pat and Burns favor the plan, Pat tells *Business Week* that Burns "did most of the work" and he deserves most of the credit.

With competing welfare proposals, Burns solicits endorsements to bolster his position: Paul McCracken, chairman of the president's Council of Economic Advisers, favors the Burns plan; Robert Mayo, director of the Bureau of the Budget, favors the Burns plan; Treasury Secretary David Kennedy favors the Burns plan; Commerce Secretary Maurice Stans favors the Burns plan. Vice President Spiro Agnew is even to the right of Burns: "By limiting aid to families with dependent children to those cases where both parents are present, I believe you would assure a better chance that the money would be spent productively. Where there is no father in the house, the mother should be given the option of either accepting work training or staying at home with the children. I want to argue most emphatically that income supplementation for families headed by a female alone gives us no reasonable assurance that the money provided for the child would be spent for the child's benefit."

But in terms of influencing the president, the key comment—actually an elaborate report—comes from Secretary of Labor George Shultz. He favors FAP, but proposes nearly doubling its cost. He wants the program to create an incentive to work. There is a cost to working—workers have to pay for transportation to and from their jobs, buy clothes, hire babysitters. In this case, Shultz argued, it doesn't make sense to tax the poor on 100 percent of their earned income. Besides this "earning disregard" (costing an extra $1 billion), Shultz also proposes an expanded program for child care and training (an extra $600 million). This program then will not be "handing out money for doing nothing." Now Nixon will be able to write in his memoirs that everyone who accepts benefits must either accept work or train for work if no suitable job is available within a reasonable distance. The bottom line, as he puts it, is "no work, no welfare."

In late July, the president heads to the Pacific, where he welcomes the Apollo 11 astronauts back to Earth after their return from the moon, and continues west around the world, visiting eight countries in nine days. His press secretary announces that on August 8, five days after he returns to Washington, he will give a major televised speech announcing his long-awaited domestic agenda. John Ehrlichman joins the trip in Bucharest to work with Nixon to tie up loose ends.

On August 6, Nixon summons his cabinet to Camp David, the presidential retreat in Maryland's Catoctin Mountains, where in

Laurel Cottage he lets them debate the Family Assistance Plan. Burns writes in his diary, "I asked numerous questions, disguised to bring out the weaknesses of the plan. I made my critical comments softly; there was no need to press; everyone knew where I stood and why, especially the President. The debate was inconsequential." However, the vice president, an opponent of FAP, tries to have the final word. As he departs Camp David, possibly to break a tie vote in the Senate, Agnew turns to Nixon, "Mr. President, if there's a tie I may call you to see if you've changed your mind."

Pat thinks Burns's questioning shows the proposal is hard to understand, has too many moving parts, is too complex to follow—all of which could be a problem when the proposal is sent to Congress. The president later tells Pat and John Price that his mind had been made up for three months, but he wanted the debate "to give people time to grasp what it was we were trying to do." Of the 12 cabinet secretaries, Nixon thinks he has the support of only Finch, Shultz, and Secretary of Defense Melvin Laird.

Every president becomes a historian of the presidency—and at this moment, Nixon feels a Lincolnesque glow.

NIXON'S ADDRESS TO
THE NATION: AUGUST 8

The president is anxious to find a name for his new domestic program. Other presidents have done well with New Deal, Fair Deal, Great Society. Three times in his address Nixon calls for a "New Federalism," but it instantly falls into the bin of forgotten brands. "There wasn't an easy label" for summing up the various parts of Nixon's domestic program, recalls White House speechwriter Lee Huebner. "They're terribly important significant and individual actions, but they're all bits and pieces in a way."

In a nationally televised address from the Oval Office on Friday, August 8, Nixon outlined the program's four main areas: "First, a complete replacement of the present welfare system; second, a comprehensive new job training and placement program; third, a revamping of the Office of Economic Opportunity; and fourth, a start on the sharing of Federal tax revenues with the States."

Nowhere has the failure of government been more tragically apparent than in its efforts to help the poor and especially in its system of public welfare.

Tonight I . . . propose that we will abolish the present welfare system and that we adopt in its place a new family assistance system. Initially, this new system will cost more than welfare. But, unlike welfare, it is designed to correct the condition it deals with and, thus, to lessen the long-range burden and cost.

Under this plan, the so-called "adult categories" of aid—aid to the aged, the blind, the disabled—would be continued, and a national minimum standard for benefits would be set, with the Federal Government contributing to its cost and also sharing the cost of additional State payments above that amount.

But the program now called "Aid to Families with Dependent Children"—the program we all normally think of when we think of "welfare"—would be done away with completely. The new family assistance system I propose in its place rests essentially on these three principles: equality of treatment across the Nation, a work requirement, and a work incentive.

Its benefits would go to the working poor, as well as the non-working; to families with dependent children headed by a father, as well as to those headed by a mother; and a basic Federal minimum would be provided, the same in every State.

What I am proposing is that the Federal Government build a foundation under the income of every American family with dependent children that cannot care for itself--and wherever in America that family may live.

For a family of four now on welfare, with no outside income, the basic Federal payment would be $1,600 a year. States could add to that amount and most States would add to it. In no case would anyone's present level of benefits be lowered. At the same time, this foundation would be one on which the family itself could build. Outside earnings would be encouraged, not discouraged. The new worker could keep the first $60 a month of outside earnings with no reduction in his benefits; and beyond that, his benefits would be reduced by only 50 cents for each dollar earned.

By the same token, a family head already employed at low wages could get a family assistance supplement; those who work would no longer be discriminated against. For example, a family of five in which the father earns $2,000 a year—which is the hard fact of life for many families in America today—would get family assistance payments of $1,260, so that they would have a total income of $3,260. A family of seven earning $3,000 a year would have its income raised to $4,360.

Thus, for the first time, the government would recognize that it has no less an obligation to the working poor than to the nonworking poor; and for the first time, benefits would be scaled in such a way that it would always pay to work.

With such incentives, most recipients who can work will want to work. This is part of the American character.

What is Pat thinking as he watches the president propose the Family Assistance Plan? This is how he answers Bernard Asbell for an article that will appear in the *New York Times* on Sunday, November 2:

> *I felt I was finally* rid of a subject. *A subject that just—that had* spoiled my life. Four—long—years *of being called awful things. The people you would most want to admire you detesting you. Being anathematized and stigmatized. And I said, "Well, the President's done* this, *and now I'm rid of it."*
>
> *You know, the libs will never forgive him. Richard Nixon has now done the final, unforgivable thing to the liberals. He's done what they wouldn't do. This was the first Presidential message on welfare in history. All previous Presidents were afraid of it and*

*tucked the subject under Social Security. . . . Now Richard Nixon
has done this. The big liberals who didn't do it—who couldn't do
it—are just shocked.* Not enough! Inadequate!

Pat's instincts are largely correct. Liberal publications are, if
not livid, at least confounded by this proposal emanating from the
Nixon White House. Ehrlichman's office compiles an analysis of
press reactions to the welfare program for the White House staff.
"The President thought you would find it interesting," reads the
note conveying a copy to Pat. The report reads, in part:

> It is no exaggeration to say that this is the one Presidential proposal
> that has met with the most immediate and widespread approval.
> Editorial columns from all regions praised the President's August 8
> speech and agreed something must be done about the welfare mess.
>
> While there was agreement that the proposal was necessary,
> there was not so much unanimity as to its adequacy or its work-
> ability. The liberal press called for more aid for the industrial-
> ized eastern states, while conservatives generally were cautious in
> assessing the ideological aspects and the fact that it would add
> $4 billion to the budget.
>
> The liberal papers were generally confounded that it was the
> "conservative" President Richard Nixon who came up with the
> welfare plan. What impressed them most was the "boldness" of
> the plan. . . . Moving to the Midwest, the *Cleveland Plain Dealer*
> sees pitfalls, but hopes that the basic reforms succeed. . . . From
> the South, there is a division of opinion—primarily based on ide-
> ology—among the metropolitan dailies. . . . The *New York Daily
> News* has queasy, uneasy thoughts—mainly that it would "create a
> pressure group of professional reliefers, eternally pushing for more
> of the taxpayers' hard-earned money and forever easier access to

the gravy train. . . ." The *New York Times* is pleased with the "overall design" of the plan, but thinks that the plan needs to be reshaped to "temper some of its present unfairness to the urban poor. . . ."

Ehrlichman's tabulators fail to include Mary McGrory's column of August 11 in the *Washington Star:*

When the match was made between staid, cautious Richard Nixon and Daniel P. Moynihan, the dashing Democratic urbanist, onlookers gave it six months at the outside. . . . And last Friday night, Moynihan was vindicated, a man whose time had come. His breakaway idea of insuring minimum incomes to poor families was presented as public policy by a conservative Republican President, one nobody ever thought would be accused of being soft on the poor.

TIME FOR CHANGE: NOVEMBER 4

The president finally has his domestic policy. Arthur Burns and Pat Moynihan sheathe their weapons. Their war over Nixon is over. Nixon is fond of Burns and fascinated by Moynihan, but he longs for quiet to return to the offices of the president. Moreover, as with all presidencies, there is a time when their needs change. Those who have been at the White House to provide ideas have provided the ideas, and now the need is to legislate and administer. Rarely are the idea people also the best people to legislate and administer.

On October 17, Nixon announces the nomination of Dr. Arthur Burns to be the next chairman of the Federal Reserve.

Two weeks later, on November 4, he announces that Dr. Daniel P. Moynihan will become counselor to the president, with cabinet rank, until he returns to Harvard at the end of 1970.

John D. Ehrlichman will be replacing both Burns and Moynihan. He becomes assistant to the president for domestic affairs. "This position will be roughly equivalent in domestic matters to the position held by Dr. Henry Kissinger in national security affairs."

Pat is not dissatisfied that within the White House it will be Ehrlichman who takes over the heavy lifting on urban affairs. Ehrlichman, a lawyer, is a practical operator with a sense of humor and probably, as Bill Safire suspects, "a closet liberal."

The question inside the Washington Beltway is whether Pat has been promoted or kicked upstairs. This is not Nixon's question, however. Haldeman explains in his diary on October 8: "Decided today to make Moynihan a Counselor to [the President] with Cabinet rank. Really best way to position him. Gets him out of operations, and into free-wheeling idea-generating, plus working as a prod to all others, good use of great talent."

Herb Klein, the communications director, recalls that "soon after Burns and Moynihan left, the White House changed distinctly and became an organization where hardball replaced political philosophy as a major consideration." But I wouldn't know firsthand because I wasn't there. On December 5, the president announces that I will be national chairman of the White House Conference on Children and Youth.

When I look back on 1969, I see the struggle between Pat and Burns as having been a gentlemen's quarrel—fencers of the épée rather than the broadsword—rare, even unique, in Washington's corridors of power. It contrasts dramatically with the foreign policy conflict between the secretary of state and the national security adviser, as described by the president in his memoirs: "Rogers felt that Kissinger was Machiavellian, deceitful, egotistical, arrogant, and insulting. Kissinger felt that Rogers was vain, uninformed, unable to keep a secret, and hopelessly dominated by the State Department bureaucracy."

Writing about these events in 1973, Pat will recall that "our debate was never nasty and, in my view, Burns was far more often correct in his forecasts than I was. An economist of formidable power, he is even more an intellectual in that singularly brilliant Middle-European Jewish tradition."

Burns too, writing in his diary on December 29, 1970, will be generous in his recollection of Pat: "Pat is wonderfully articulate and lends charm even to trite phrases—which are fewer in his case than in that of any member of Nixon's staff or Cabinet. . . . While I think Moynihan misled the President badly on the welfare problem, something will be lost when he is gone."

As Pat will write in *The Politics of a Guaranteed Income,* his 1973 book about the welfare reform debates in the Nixon White House, "There are no villains in this book."

◄► PLANTING GREATNESS

Presidents are forced to make key decisions more often than acting of their own free will. They are pushed or pulled by world events, by the courts, by Congress, by their political party, by interest groups, by public opinion. Yet none of these forces accounts for Richard Nixon's welfare reform proposal: quite the contrary, a majority of Republicans oppose his plan, as his vice president keeps reminding him, and the voters that would be most aided by the Family Assistance Plan are not his voters, nor are they likely to be.

Why then does Nixon propose a policy that Michael Harrington, a leading socialist writer on poverty in America, calls "the most radical idea since the New Deal"?

The question baffles enough observers that A. James Reichley, in his book *Conservatives in an Age of Change* (Brookings, 1981), lists eight suggestions that have been made over the years, including "Nixon wanted to give a victory to Finch," the cabinet officer with whom he had the longest and closest history, and "Milton Friedman's identification with the negative income tax persuaded Nixon that it must have some conservative attributes."

Start with an unassailable fact: only Pat gets Nixon to FAP. No Moynihan on the White House staff, no FAP. This does not guarantee that Nixon will embrace FAP, only that it will be raised and debated at the highest levels. Arthur Burns is a forceful opponent, and Nixon is careful to balance the time he gives each side. In fact, the president's daily logs show that Burns spent more time in meetings with Nixon—but this is because of Burns's additional involvement in economic policy.

However, Pat is by far the more skilled player; he is even liked by Haldeman and Ehrlichman, the so-called Berlin Wall, while Burns is not. Unlike his White House colleagues, he knows how to engage reporters, although this is only marginally useful in what will decide the contest.

Making the case for FAP is exceedingly difficult for Pat. For every argument he makes about what welfare reform could do, Burns challenges him to prove it. Negative income tax experiments in New Jersey, Iowa, and North Carolina, for instance, are too small and too inconclusive. Pat too is a scholar and understands the difference between fact and opinion. His grand offer to Nixon is of hope. Aren't we a country that can provide a better future for children in the families that have been left behind?

But a massive unproven idea is an offer of great risk. There are times when presidents have to take great risks. For Nixon, this is not one of them. Burns's advice offers safety, incremental change in a time when the president has major concerns abroad, limited money to spend, and a past record of negative statements on government-run domestic programs. This is sound presidential advising based importantly on the adviser's belief that he understands the advisee, which, it turns out, he doesn't. "Does he lack the courage to face me?" Burns eventually asks himself in his diary. "Have I misjudged Nixon? Does he have real convictions?"

These are not questions that Pat has to ask. He never supported Nixon in an election. He is at the White House because he is of the other party. He is willing to reserve judgment on the president. But he has very strong views on the presidency. For every American there is a "personal presidency" shaped by one's own experiences and the experiences that one shares with those of the same generation. Studies of political socialization show that a child's first recognition of government in the person of the president comes at about third grade and becomes more defined by late high school. Pat was born in 1927, a poor Irish Catholic boy from New York. Franklin D. Roosevelt became president in 1933 and was still president when Pat enlisted in the navy in 1944. The presidency, Pat's personal presidency, is a leader who successfully brings his country through a Great Depression and a Just War. It is a heroic model.

Suddenly, Pat is given an opportunity to try to shape a president in office. This is not the way presidential assistants are supposed to think about their time in the White House. But Pat Moynihan has created himself, as someday a biographer will explain. Moreover, his charm, wit, and intelligence are uniquely suited to the assignment he has given himself.

Aspire to greatness, which is really Pat's message to Nixon, may be okay for athletes and actors, but for presidents there must be a code word. That word is history (historic, historical). Even something as mundane as Nixon changing some boxes on an organizational chart becomes, in Pat's pronouncement, "the first time in the history of the American Republic that the regional boundaries of the major domestic programs will be coterminous."

From his very first "For the President" memo, Pat is telling Nixon that he could be or would be or is being a *historic* president. From the outside, this might look like rank flattery. But it doesn't look like flattery to a president. (Henry Kissinger also understands this.) Doesn't every president aspire to greatness? No. Theodore Roosevelt did, but not William Howard Taft. FDR, not Herbert Hoover. Ronald Reagan, not George H. W. Bush. What presidents do, as they swear the oath of office, is "to the best of my Ability, preserve, protect and defend the Constitution of the United States." Probably fewer than half of all presidents enter the White House with their sights set on historic greatness.

Did Nixon? Putting international affairs aside, I don't think so. I had spent hundreds of hours in conversation with Nixon between 1961 and 1965, and I deeply admired his analytical ability. But I never saw the sort of future thrust that I associated with greatness. Nor, I'm sure, did Pat when he signed on with Nixon during the 1968 transition. Nor could Pat have known why he was going to succeed and Burns fail in the welfare reform debate.

ON FERTILE GROUND

Unknown at the time, at least to me, is the degree to which Pat recognizes that Nixon's childhood would be fertile ground on which to plant welfare reform. Both Pat and Nixon had known poverty in childhood. It was a very different kind of poverty, in different places and at different times—but poverty all the same. Some very successful men love to tell Dickensian tales of hard times as kids. But this is not the way of either Pat or Nixon, and I doubt it was ever a subject of prolonged conversation between them. When he is profiled by the media, Pat will oblige with several anecdotes—shining shoes on 42nd Street, helping in his mother's Hell's Kitchen saloon—but this is as far as he will go. His was a complicated poverty.

Nixon, as a seeker of public office, also has a small number of growing-up-in-poverty stories. This is why there is something different and special about Nixon's speech of December 13, 1970.

The president is at the Sheraton Park Hotel in Washington giving the opening address to the White House Conference on Children. I am on the stage as the national chairman, but am more attentive to how the audience of social workers and school administrators is going to react to a president they don't much like than to his credit-claiming remarks:

> On August 11, 1969, over a year ago, I proposed that for the first time in American history we in this great, rich country establish a floor under the income of every American family with children. We called it the family assistance plan. It has, in turn, been called by others the most important piece of domestic legislation to be introduced in Congress in two generations. In terms of consequences for children, I think it can be fairly said to be the most important piece of social legislation in the history of this Nation.

At this point the tone changes: he is no longer giving a quasi-campaign speech. I had written a lot of words for Richard Nixon over the years, but never anything like this:

> I remember back in the Depression years . . . how deeply I felt about the plight of those people my own age who used to come into my father's store when they couldn't pay the bill, because their fathers were out of work, and how this seemed to separate them from others in our school.
>
> None of us had any money in those days, but those in families where there were no jobs and there was nothing but the little that relief then offered suffered from more than simply going without. What they suffered was a hurt to their pride that many carried with them for the rest of their lives.
>
> I also remember my older brother. He had tuberculosis for 5 years. The hospital, the doctor bills were more than we could afford.
>
> In the 5 years before he died, my mother never bought a new dress. We were poor by today's standards, and I suppose we were poor even by Depression standards.

But the wonder of it was that we didn't know it. Somehow my mother and father, with their love, their pride, their courage, and their self-sacrifice, were able to create a spirit of self-respect in our family so that we had no sense of being inferior to others who had more.

Today's welfare child is not so fortunate. His family may have enough to get by on, and, as a matter of fact, they may have even more in a material sense than many of us had in those Depression years. But no matter how much pride and courage his parents have, he knows they are poor and he can feel that soul-stifling patronizing attitude that follows the dole.

Early the next morning, deep in sleep, the ringing phone wakes me. "The President is calling."

Nixon comes on the line. "Steve, why isn't my speech on the front page in the *Times?*"

"I haven't yet seen the *Times,* Mr. President. What's the byline?"

He tells me.

"That explains it," I say. "The *Times* reporter should have been Nan Robertson, but her husband's in the hospital. It's from the AP and the *Times* isn't going to lead the paper with a wire service story."

This satisfies him. I ask, "How was the *Post?*"

"Okay," he says and hangs up. His judgment, obviously, is that the *Washington Post* is not in the same league with the *Times.*

When I'm more awake, I find out that Ray Price had written a draft for the children's conference speech, but the president couldn't sleep and at 4:30 a.m. he began to rewrite. The words were Nixon's.

A YEAR OF DEPARTURES
1970

UNFINISHED BUSINESS

With the unveiling of the Family Assistance Plan, Pat can finally turn his focus to unfinished business. On the morning of November 22, 1963, he had been at the White House to discuss his proposal for turning Pennsylvania Avenue between the Capitol and the White House into a grand thoroughfare. President Kennedy had planned to present it to congressional leaders on his return from Dallas.

Following President Kennedy's assassination, honoring him with a redesigned Pennsylvania Avenue becomes Pat's obsession.

On May 29, 1970, on what would have been President Kennedy's 53rd birthday, Pat writes to Jacqueline Kennedy Onassis: "On behalf of President Nixon I went over to Arlington Cemetery this morning and laid a wreath." He tells her about his Pennsylvania Avenue meeting at the White House in 1963. "I have understood that this was one of a very few items on a list of things you felt he would have wanted finished, which you left with President Johnson. Anyway, I have stayed with it these many years. With any luck before the fortnight is out we will have a formal Presidential proposal and a bill."

Pat's "fortnight" stretches for over two more years. Some Washington community leaders oppose the project as "a Monument Plan, not a People Plan . . . largely irrelevant to the needs of the people of the city." There are also businesses that don't want to be uprooted. Pat recruits Nixon to make a daytime walking tour of the avenue to express his support for the Moynihan plan. Finally, in October 1972, Congress approves, and Nixon signs into law, the Pennsylvania Avenue Development Corporation.

IN APRIL, Pat returns to Brussels for the second meeting of NATO's Committee on the Challenges of Modern Society (CCMS). He reports back to the president:

> I don't wish to sound like a caricature of a second secretary in a British embassy, but a certain ambiguity is unavoidable. Forthrightness would be misleading. The dilemma is simple. The CCMS is underway. Things are getting done. Much faster than anyone had a right to expect. However, so far, everything that has happened has been the result of American push. . . . Almost all the NATO countries are taking part in one or more of these projects. . . . The English are serious sort of, but in a dawdling way. The French have been embarrassed into taking on the subject of regional development, and are proceeding at about the pace regional development proceeds. . . . You should not underestimate what you have already achieved. One of the reasons the Allies have had trouble getting started is that none of them was organized to think about environmental problems. . . . The big question is whether some kind of enduring North Atlantic policy can grow out of this initiative.

Pat's caution is more justified than his optimism. CCMS is eventually merged with another NATO committee. According to Luke Nichter, a scholar of Nixon's European policies, "The CCMS was successful in helping to hold together NATO during a time of rising isolation at home and increasing concern from allies on the need for a costly defense alliance. At the same time, the CCMS did not become a sweeping new American vision for NATO."

PAT RETAINS INVOLVEMENT in one policy area, education, where he is a member of the White House working group, and where Checker Finn will be at hand to run interference when necessary. This will result in two presidential messages to Congress on elementary and secondary education (March 3) and higher education (March 19). The first message emphasizes doing research into what works rather than throwing more money at the problem. Brookings scholars Robert Hartman and Alice Rivlin testify before a Senate subcommittee that the administration is proposing "bold reform," but "on an inadequate budget." The *New York Times* accuses the president of offering "a pledge to a drowning man that help will come as soon as the experts find out why he is swimming so poorly." In the second message, Nixon proposes Pat's idea for a new National Foundation for Higher Education. Pat's two governing themes, as Checker will explain in his book *Education and the Presidency* (Lexington Books, 1977), are an "opportunity for students to attend college without regard to their economic condition and a noninterventionist federal stance toward higher education institutions that does not let Washington's dollars get too much in the way of academic self-determination."

IN HIS SECOND year in the White House, Pat assumes a function he had resisted in 1969 and becomes the White House's intellectual-in-residence, offering the president outreach to thinkers and the academic world. He tells Nixon what is worth reading and who is worth meeting: Sidney Hook, James Q. Wilson,

David Riesman, Aaron Wildavsky, Daniel Bell, Irving Kristol. His memos even provide thumbnail sketches for the president: "Lionel Trilling. Columbia. English literature. The leading academic literary scholar of the nation. A man of transcendent rationality, and fierce opposition to authoritarian trends everywhere." This is not a front page assignment; still, it is fun, as it had been for Arthur Schlesinger Jr. in the Kennedy White House. (When Pat leaves the White House later in the year, Nixon's inner circle will consider candidates—such as University of California sociologist Robert Nisbet—to succeed Pat in the thinker-without-portfolio role. But ultimately Pat will not be replaced.)

GIVEN PAT'S ACHIEVEMENTS in 1969 and his enjoyable new tasks in 1970, his last year in the Nixon White House before returning to Harvard should be a victory lap. It is not.

"Benign Neglect"

On March 1, the following headline appears on the front page of the *New York Times:* "'Benign Neglect' on Race Is Proposed by Moynihan."

The two words are from a confidential memo that Pat sends to the president on January 16. The memo is intended to be "a general assessment of the position of Negroes at the end of the first year of your administration." It begins, "In quantitative terms, which are reliable, the American Negro is making extraordinary progress. In political terms, somewhat less reliable, this would also appear to be true. In each case, however, there would seem to be counter-currents. . . ."

The complete "benign neglect" paragraph reads, "The time may have come when the issue of race could benefit from a period of 'benign neglect.' The subject has been too much talked about. The forum has been too much taken over to hysterics, paranoids, and boodlers on all sides. We may need a period in which Negro progress continues and racial rhetoric fades." As has been his practice for the past year, Nixon forwards Pat's memo to the vice president, the cabinet, and key White House aides. The president makes "extensive written notations" on his copy. Over the words "benign neglect," he writes "I agree." This is the disaster waiting to happen.

Pat attempts to track down the recipients. "It would be a grievous breach of the President's privacy if these comments were to become public." But he discovers how vast is the distribution—not just those who got the memo from the president, but those who got it from those who got it. At HEW, for example, Bob Finch replies that he has passed along his copy to "Mr. Veneman, Mr. Butler, Mr. Panetta, Mr. Farmer, and to the speech writing group."

Inevitably, the memo (without the president's annotations) is leaked to the press. Leakers leak to do harm, or to help, or merely to show a reporter how important they are to have such valuable information. In this case, neither leaker nor motive is known. Pat's two words—clear in context—soon acquire a life of their own. Pat regrets their use. Had he known the document would be made public, he tells a press conference on March 2, he would have added "a long historical footnote. . . . It was the Earl of Durham who coined the phrase in an 1839 report to the Colonial Office of the United Kingdom, explaining that Canada was progressing in its capacity of self-government."

In what resembles a replay of the Moynihan Report fiasco in 1965, Pat knows he has been badly hurt. Whitney Young of the Urban League declares, "Moynihan's memo is one more example of a systematic effort on both the federal and state level to wipe out all the gains made in the 1950s and 1960s." Pat offers to resign. "Of course, I refused his offer," recalls Nixon.

The president "wants me to clamp down on leaks," writes Bob Haldeman in his notes. "Problem is how."

Escalation of the Vietnam War

"I never had any illusions about the shattering effect a decision to go into Cambodia would have on public opinion at home," Nixon will write in his memoirs.

Addressing the nation on April 30, the president announces: "In cooperation with the armed forces of South Vietnam, attacks are being launched this week to clean out major enemy sanctuaries on the Cambodian-Vietnam border." Although the sanctuaries are not in Vietnam, Nixon says that "this is not an invasion of Cambodia." He is not wrong about "the shattering effect" of his decision. The White House is now under siege, surrounded by a ring of buses tightly lined front-to-back. Trucks are unloading troops from the Third Army in the Executive Office Building next to the White House. Three of Kissinger's top aides resign in protest, as well as a young Yale graduate, Art Klebanoff, who had joined Pat's staff in September.

Nixon visits the Pentagon on May 1 and, during a conversation with a group of employees who have gathered in a corridor to greet him, says, "You see these bums, you know, blowing up the campuses. Listen, the boys that are on the college campuses today are the luckiest people in the world, going to the greatest universities, and here they are burning up the books." "Bums" makes the headlines. On May 4, four students are killed by National Guard soldiers at Kent State University in Ohio. Nixon's Kent

State statement is read by his press secretary at his regular afternoon briefing: "This should remind us all once again that when dissent turns to violence, it invites tragedy." Is Nixon approving the National Guard's actions? Vice President Agnew describes the protesters as "choleric young intellectuals and tired, embittered elders." Journalist Clark R. Mollenhoff, who is serving as a special counsel to the president, calls the student protesters "thugs and outlaws."

"My views on the war are well known to you," Pat tells Nixon, "and have been from the outset of my service to you." Essentially he sees the war as misguided, rather than in the moral terms preferred by the "dove" wing of his party. As such, he can coexist with Nixon as long as he feels Nixon's primary aim is to end the war. If Nixon pursues "a high risk" strategy, "I do not contest your judgment." But "it seems absolutely necessary that you call a halt to the vulgar partisanship and hysterical demagoguery of people theoretically on your team."

Pat writes the president, "I doubt anybody around here quite understands how menacing the administration has seemed to students and faculties alike." Nixon is about to have a press conference, and Pat asks him to say that "the action of the National Guard [at Kent State] is utterly to be deplored . . . [and to] retract the statement about 'bums.'" Neither of Nixon's answers gives Pat much comfort: "As far as the Vice President is concerned, he will answer for anything he has said. . . . I shall not do that. . . . And when students on university campuses burn buildings . . . then I think 'bums' is perhaps too kind a word to apply to that kind of person."

The next day Pat tells the president, "Yesterday in Cambridge the [Students for a Democratic Society] announced that my house would be burned during the night. The University asked my family to 'evacuate' and they, in effect, went into hiding." Godfrey Hodgson, a British friend of the Moynihans, will vividly describe the scene in his biography of Pat, *The Gentleman from New York* (Houghton Mifflin, 2000):

> Liz Moynihan remembers all too well what it felt like. [She] called the schools and sent word for the children to go to a friend's house on the other side of the campus. Then she got hold of two of the babysitters, Harvard students who lived on their top floor. They pushed the furniture into the middle of the room and covered it with dust sheets. She grabbed the things that seemed most precious: three boxes of [Pat's] manuscript, which she took to the Cambridge Trust Company for safety; photos of the kids and their favorite pets. Then she and the babysitters made a huge peace sign and left it on the pile of furniture. Finally she told the students to leave the house and mingle with the crowd. . . . In the end, the Harvard Divinity School freshmen faced down the radicals, and neither the burning nor the trashing took place.

Pat's two conflicting worlds—the academy and government— are becoming increasingly entangled. In a letter dated May 11, sent "special delivery," underlined "personal and confidential," Wassily Leontief, a professor of economics at Harvard who will later receive the Nobel Prize, writes Pat:

DEAR MOYNIHAN:

I take the liberty of writing to you not because I have a close personal relationship with you but just because I have not.

Whatever happens in the next few weeks and months, the cleavage between those who support the present administration in Washington and those who oppose it not only on political but also on intellectual and human grounds is bound to grow. The last bridges between the two shores are already burning.

I would be very sorry to see you remain with Henry [Kissinger] on the other shore and hit the trail to Texas [as did MIT professor Walt Rostow after serving on President Johnson's staff]. Hence I urge you to resign (with a bang) and come back to Cambridge before it is too late. Now—and I mean not next week—you would be received with open arms.

Pat resigns quietly—not with a bang—in a private meeting with Nixon on May 13. The president had honored him and become his friend. He says he would like to leave for Harvard on July 1. Nixon asks, and Pat agrees, that he stay a bit longer to help get FAP through the Senate. Kissinger too must make a similar decision. After a contentious meeting with a group of Harvard professors who visit him in the Situation Room, Kissinger chooses to stay. "The wounds would have to be healed after the war was over," he concludes. When Pat finally leaves at the end of 1970, he will receive a note from Kissinger on January 12, 1971: "As you depart from the ivory tower of the White House out into the cold, cruel world of the academia, rest assured that you can always turn to your friends here for sympathy and for a detached intellectual assessment of the problems you are wrestling with there. I, for one, will not fail you."

Defeat of the Family Assistance Plan

Pat's final months in the White House end as they began—in a blaze of memoranda to the president. The focus now is to urge the president to push the Senate to support the Family Assistance Plan:

You are meeting this afternoon with a group of Southern Senators. If the opportunity arises you might want to mention to them the importance of FAP to the South.

It would be enormously helpful if you could call Ribicoff and Bennett. Ribicoff is slightly sensitive that the radicals seem to be taking credit for his work. Bennett is slightly sensitive that he may be going too far.

The Blue Lake ceremony. Indians will be major benefactors of FAP. Senator Harris will be there with his wife LaDonna, an Indian. A word to him to get cracking would help.

If you can make any calls, you might do so in the following order of priority: One, Senator Jordan; Two, Senator Hansen; Three, Senator Fannin; Four, Senator Miller; Five, Senator Bennett.

"The principal point that you have to make with the Republican members is that you want *the bill. They are telling each other that you really don't know what is in it. Only you can persuade them otherwise, and ask their support on grounds of party loyalty.*

The Senate Finance Committee could not be a more difficult venue to make the case for the Family Assistance Plan. As Pat explains, it is "a committee dominated by Democrats representing Southern states where FAP would have its greatest impact on the social order, and Republicans representing Western states where welfare [is] a minimal problem, and reform a marginal concern." Six of the ten Democrats are from the South. The position of the chairman, Russell Long of Louisiana, is not to pay people not to work. The Republicans are from Arizona, Utah, Idaho, and

Wyoming. The only eastern Republican on the committee is John Williams of Delaware, the ranking minority member, whose primary concern, in Pat's judgment, "is that citizens derive as little financial gain as possible from government, whether by theft, welfare, bribery, or whatever." Moreover, Williams has announced that he will not be running for reelection and will not be needing any more help from his party.

Nevertheless, in September, when the heat over the Cambodian incursion has died down, Nixon turns his attention to trying to influence the Finance Committee. An Air Force plane takes five members and their wives to San Diego as the president's guests at a state dinner for the president of Mexico. Another senator joins them from Arizona. Marine helicopters fly them up to San Clemente, the president's "Western White House," where the senators meet with the president while Mrs. Nixon takes the wives on a tour.

Finally, having stalled as much as possible, the committee votes on November 20, and FAP is defeated in a 10-5 vote. Seven Democrats join three Republicans in voting against it. (Democrat Vance Hartke of Indiana did not vote.) Pat thinks this is an "example of people letting the best become the enemy of the good. . . . Senators who preferred nothing to something they regarded as less than perfect." In a *Washington Post* op-ed, Alice Rivlin's explanation of what happened is that "the 'good guys' appear to have gone berserk." The Nixon administration's welfare reform, "while far from perfect and much too small, is the first really progressive step in this difficult area in many years. A President who is inching in the right direction is a poor target for the liberal, especially when moving faster would take more money than anyone thinks there is."

David Broder of the *Washington Post* offers a different explanation. In the run-up to the Finance Committee's vote, he tells

Pat, "The Democrats would not dare kill it on their own. Rather they expect the Republicans to do so, and they will then be in a position to blame the President!" In the end, Pat concludes, "Williams killed FAP." Had Lyndon Johnson been president and needed Democratic votes, he would have had them. Nixon needs Republican votes; he tries, but he is no Johnson when it comes to squeezing senators. The president will continue to lobby, but essentially FAP dies with the November 20 vote in the Finance Committee. And anyway, Nixon will soon become consumed with winning reelection.

AN UNEXPECTED INVITATION

On Saturday, June 6, while at Camp David with his family, Nixon has what seems to be a random thought in that it doesn't appear to emerge from any need or desire. He calls Haldeman: "Consider Moynihan for UN!" Haldeman replies, "Good idea." Nixon's ambassador to the United Nations is a distinguished diplomat, Charles Yost. There is no indication that the administration is displeased with Yost, nor is Yost thought to be displeased with the job.

Why Moynihan? Why the UN? Why now? Presidents and their inner circles love, for real or just for fun, to strategize moving players around the political chessboard that is the federal government. The U.S. ambassador to the United Nations seems to be a job that can fit the resume of any intelligent person, with or without diplomatic experience. Jobs of this description are hard to find. But Pat is soon going back to Harvard, on schedule and without a fuss. He has not asked for another position. One notion is that the UN is a consolation prize for not making Pat the secretary of health, education, and welfare after Finch's departure in June. (Elliot Richardson will get that job.) The rap on Bob Finch is that he was too liberal and too deficient as a manager, so why turn to Pat who is even more liberal and even less a manager?

The answer may be both simpler and more complex. Richard Nixon, outside of his family, has few deeply felt friendships. This is a fact it doesn't take a biographer to uncover. Moreover, presidents, it is said, do not make friends, only supplicants. To the degree that he is able, Richard Nixon truly feels befriended by Pat. This goes beyond liking Pat's skills as an educator and an entertainer. It is about loyalty, the commodity that Nixon holds in highest regard. Pat's commitment—as a liberal, a Democrat, and a Harvard professor—has probably been more tested than that of any other person in the administration. Nixon believes in rewards, just as he believes in the obverse.

On June 8, the president meets with Pat and asks him if he'd like to be ambassador to the United Nations. According to Haldeman's notes, "Pat is pleased with the offer, and will consider." On August 15, Haldeman reports that Pat has "agreed to take UN post in January." Going to the United Nations as America's spokesman to the world is immensely attractive to Pat. Returning to Harvard is perhaps losing some luster, as it is not clear which department wants him.

At the White House, Pat is quietly advising Len Garment on problems relating to desegregation as schools in the South open in September for the new school year. Strangely, the UN appointment has not been announced and Yost has still not been notified. On Tuesday, November 17, at 4 p.m., Pat and Nixon, according to Pat's notes, "talked at some length about the UN and the President's desire to somehow turn it into a more active organization." Pat then goes to Acapulco for a conference on housing. On Friday, November 20, the Family Assistance Plan loses the key vote in the Senate Finance Committee. Also, the *Boston Globe* leaks the unauthorized story that Pat will succeed Yost at the UN. Pat returns to Washington on Sunday.

What happens on Monday Pat explains to journalist Richard Meryman:

> *I went out to dinner and asked Steve Hess to be my deputy. I went home and between the time I got into the elevator on the first floor and got out on the fifth floor, I decided, I don't want to be around this Administration anymore. And I called my wife, Liz, who was miserable about the prospect of the UN, and I said, "I'm not going to stay. I'm going."*

Pat will never mention to me this conversation in which I became a part of a disturbing cross-current in his life. Nor will I say anything to him about it in the 33 years that remain of our deep friendship.

A person close to Pat and the UN decision writes to him on November 25:

> You put first things first, as you had to do, and as was the right thing to do, even if you remained torn to the end. And still are. The UN is a far sturdier creature—however ailing it may be—than a family and in the end I must respect a man who, when confronted with those two calls, picks the one that depends on *him*. And, whether he knows it or not, the one that he depends on. There are times when the right thing to do is not the beguiling thing to do. And I know you won't deny that many things about the UN post were beguiling, not least the President's own firm interest in you.

Four days after my dinner with Pat, he writes Nixon the following letter:

Dear Mr. President:

After a weekend of torment I have concluded that I must not go to the United Nations. My reasons are varied, but conclusive.

I fear my family simply could not take the strain. I have been away for two years. They have expected to resume a normal life and the prospect of not doing so has been a profound shock. For me to go forward with our plans nonetheless would be an act of callousness or worse.

What is more, I am penniless. When I came down here I had assets of some $60,000. These are now gone. Bills mount. It would be a grave mistake to suppose I could somehow manage the UN ambassadorship in such financial condition.

It is also clear to me that neither Bill Rogers nor Henry Kissinger really wants a change at the UN. They would have every reason not to. It would be foolish of me not to see this, and foolhardy to ignore it. In Secretary Rogers's case, the fact that the move leaked makes it doubly difficult for him. Ambassador Yost has been done a disservice for which, ultimately, I am responsible.

Finally, I am deeply depressed by the decision of the liberal Democrats to kill Family Assistance. I had hoped your administration would teach them something about the bases of political and social stability. I fear it has not, and now will not. I conclude I had best leave government and start writing again. . . .

It would be beyond me just at this moment to express adequately my respect for what you have done, my gratitude for the way I have been treated, and the extent of my wishes for your success.

Haldeman tells Pat that the president "understands," and he wants "critiques and suggestions from him as he has done all along." White House press secretary Ron Ziegler announces that although widely reported otherwise, Pat is returning to Harvard as originally planned. Ziegler does not deny that Pat's UN appointment was once planned, but "changes are not changes until the announcement is made from the White House." Nixon offers the UN job to the only black member of the U.S. Senate, Edward Brooke of Massachusetts, a Republican. He declines. Texas congressman George H. W. Bush, who has just lost his race for the U.S. Senate, then successfully lobbies to go to the UN.

Back at Harvard, Pat stays connected to Nixon. In the fall of 1972, the president puts him on the U.S. Delegation to the UN General Assembly. It is a part-time and mainly honorific post, yet Pat finds serious subjects, particularly on the condition of Soviet Jewry. As a paid consultant, he also comes regularly to Washington to chat with Nixon.

Restoring his bank balance is a work in progress. DuPont pays Pat $2,500 for a private dinner with the executive committee. "I never speak to a commercial group for less than $1,000," he responds to an inquiry from AT&T, "and rarely for that. We are in a market in this respect, and I maximize my position as best I can."

After two years at home in Cambridge, Pat asks Harvard for another leave of absence. This time it is to accept Nixon's offer to be ambassador to India, where he remains with his family from early 1973 to early 1975.

It is from the American Embassy in New Delhi that I receive the following cable on January 4, 1974:

```
1. I read by our morning press file that under
the new Supplemental Security Income Program
three million poor Americans who are aged,
blind or disabled have now begun to receive
```

> regular income supplements from the federal
> government.
>
>   2. We did not get everything Family Assis-
> tance envisioned, but we did get this, and as
> no one else will, we may as well take note of
> it with one another. It is no small thing. Hap-
> pier New Year.

Pat's cable concludes our story with a scrap of irony that he would have liked. The Family Assistance Plan that he had brought to the Nixon White House in 1969, and which was defeated in the Senate in 1970, was reconsidered by the next Congress, 1971–72. This time the strategy of Senate Finance Committee chairman Russell Long was to counter FAP with Supplemental Security Income (SSI), which would federalize three discrete programs run by the states—Aid to the Blind, Aid to the Permanently and Totally Disabled, and Aid to the Elderly. Now, under the new legislation, these programs would be run by the Social Security Administration; in addition, Social Security benefits would be significantly raised and indexed to the rate of inflation.

In late October 1972, a few days before his reelection, Nixon hailed the passage of "landmark legislation that will end many old inequities and will provide a new uniform system of well-earned benefits for older Americans, the blind, and the disabled." More than 40 years later, historians Edward D. Berkowitz and Larry DeWitt will note, "Few people recalled it at the time, but the 1972 legislation marked the very apex of the American welfare state."

FAP's legacy then? "We may as well take note," Pat might have cabled, "of the success within our failure." He never regretted his two years among the Republicans. "During those first few years of Nixon, there was some damn good government."

AFTERWORD

So end the years 1969 and 1970 of Daniel Patrick Moynihan's tenure as an aide in Richard Nixon's White House. For the players in the story, this is their afterword.

RICHARD M. NIXON won reelection in 1972, but not by seven-tenths of a percentage point as he had in 1968. He won over 60 percent of the popular vote, losing only Massachusetts and the District of Columbia to Democrat George McGovern. Also in 1972, five men, paid by the Nixon campaign, were arrested while breaking into the Democratic headquarters at a Washington building named Watergate. Nixon denied knowledge until a taping system within the White House eventually produced a "smoking gun" tape that proved otherwise. The Watergate scandal ultimately encompassed a wide range of other illegalities. But the crimes relating to covering up Watergate were what brought down the president and his top aides.

H. R. (Bob) Haldeman and John Ehrlichman were tried on counts of perjury, conspiracy, and obstruction of justice. Each spent 18 months in prison. John Mitchell, who had resigned as attorney general to manage Nixon's reelection campaign, was also convicted for his involvement in Watergate and served 19 months in prison.

Nixon resigned the office of the presidency on August 9, 1974. Post-presidency, he wrote nine books almost exclusively centered on international relations. He died on April 22, 1994, age 81. He was buried on the grounds of the Nixon Library, Yorba Linda, California, beside his wife, Pat, in a ceremony that included eulogies by President Bill Clinton and former secretary of state Henry Kissinger. In attendance were also former presidents Ford, Carter, Reagan, George H. W. Bush, and their wives.

DANIEL PATRICK MOYNIHAN returned to Harvard from India in 1975, and within months was packing again, this time to move to New York as President Gerald Ford's ambassador to the United Nations, the job that had so intrigued him when Nixon first offered it in 1970. Henry Kissinger was now secretary of state and liked the idea of employing Pat's sense of moral outrage—until he didn't like it. Much of Pat's eight months at the UN was spent opposing a UN resolution declaring Zionism to be a form of racism.

Pat had formed a bond in the White House with Leonard Garment, who was now the U.S. representative to the United Nations Human Rights Commission, a part-time assignment in Geneva, but with latitude to assist Pat in New York. In the world of professional diplomacy, however, Kissinger soon saw the downside to their excess of passion. Pat resigned in February 1976, returning to Harvard once again. But his UN work had made him a national celebrity, and in November 1976 he was elected as a Democrat to the U.S. Senate from New York. While working for Nixon and Ford, Pat always made clear that he remained a Democrat.

Still, it felt good to be politically home again. He was reelected in 1982, 1988, and 1994, choosing not to run in 2000, the year in which President Clinton awarded him the Presidential Medal of Freedom, the honor he had helped resurrect decades earlier. He remains the only Democratic senator from New York to serve four full six-year terms.

Also in 2000, Congress designated a parcel of land along the redeveloped Pennsylvania Avenue, near the intersection with 13th Street, N.W., in Washington, D.C., as Daniel Patrick Moynihan Place, in recognition of his role in formulating the Pennsylvania Avenue Development Corporation.

He died on March 26, 2003, at the age of 76, and is buried at Arlington National Cemetery, just down the hill to the left of the gravesite of John F. Kennedy.

ARTHUR BURNS'S struggles continued as chairman of the Federal Reserve. John Ehrlichman, who had emerged as the head of the White House's domestic operation, remembered, "Nixon was determined to control the Fed while maintaining the image of its independence from all politicians, including himself. He went as far as he could, lecturing—even scolding—Arthur Burns about what the Fed must do to free up the money supply."

Burns's disappointment with Nixon became a theme of his diary, as on November 5, 1971: "The President's preoccupation with the election frightens me. Is there anything that he would not do to further his reelection?" Meeting with Nixon two weeks before his 1972 victory, Burns saw "a man who feels that he finally has not only position in the world, but great power as well. But I see no indication as yet that, apart from foreign field, he has the slightest idea what he wants to use the power for; unless it be to nourish some old grudges and prejudices."

When President Jimmy Carter did not reappoint Burns in 1978, he made his intellectual home at the American Enterprise Institute in Washington. President Reagan appointed him U.S. ambassador to West Germany in 1981, a post he held until mid-1985. Dr. Burns died on June 26, 1987, age 82. His memorial service at AEI included tributes from Richard Nixon and George Shultz.

MARTIN ANDERSON remained at the White House in 1970 after Burns went to the Fed, but his relationship with Ehrlichman was frigid. In 1971, he found his intellectual home at the Hoover Institution at Stanford University, where he is now the Keith and Jan Hurlbut Senior Fellow. He returned to the White House in 1981–82 as President Reagan's chief domestic policy adviser and has since become a leading scholar on the Reagan presidency as well as on Reagan's pre-presidential career.

STEPHEN HESS, on assuming the national chairmanship of the White House Conference on Children and Youth, a decennial event founded by President Theodore Roosevelt in 1909, decided that it would not be possible to adequately focus on the demands of youth and the needs of children in one conference. Instead, with the president's permission, a White House Conference on Children was held in 1970 and a White House Conference on Youth in 1971, with different agendas and different constituencies. He left the administration in January 1972 to become a senior fellow at the Brookings Institution, where he remains except for various tours teaching at universities or advising governments.

There were four key people on the Moynihan-Hess staff at the White House in 1969. Rarely do the young aides who do the heavy lifting get the recognition or appreciation they deserve. What follows is meant, belatedly, to reflect their contributions to the success of the Urban Affairs Office and their subsequent achievements.

RICHARD BLUMENTHAL, 22 years old in 1969, had been Pat's student at Harvard. His senior thesis was published as "The Bureaucracy: Antipoverty and the Community Action Program," one of five case studies (the other four by political science professors) in *American Political Institutions and Public Policy* (Little, Brown and Company, 1969). Before joining Pat's team, he had been a *Washington Post* intern and had taught for six months at Ballou High School in the impoverished Anacostia section of Washington, D.C.

The first job Pat gave him was to link the White House to the District of Columbia government, a small yet sensitive piece of Pat's portfolio. Presidents at the time even appointed members of the Washington City Council. The White House's involvement in governing this 70 percent African American city could have, at any time, led to the following nightmare headline: "(White) 22-Year-Old Overseer of (Black) Capital City." But nothing like this ever happened. Who taught Dick to work so delicately without controversy? (Certainly not Pat.)

Dick got another job of considerable usefulness when Don Rumsfeld became the director of the Office of Economic Opportunity and Pat assigned him to smooth Rumsfeld's path from legislative to executive government. "One of the most able guys I've ever met," said Rumsfeld. After the 1970 White House changeover, Dick enlisted in the Marine Corps for a six-month tour of duty. Suddenly, on July 14, 1970, headlines and photographs appeared in all major newspapers: "Blumenthal, 24, Turns Down Offer to Take Over VISTA." Volunteers in Service to America, a sort of domestic Peace Corps, was a part of Rumsfeld's OEO and had been without a director since mid-1968. Rumsfeld had made the offer to Dick, which found its way into the news because of Dick's habit—dating back to his days as chairman of the *Harvard Crimson*—of frequently seeking the career advice of friends. The leak had an anti-administration angle (the *New York Times*'s subhead read "Liberal Reported to Decline VISTA Post Because He Disagrees with Policies").

Dick denied this in a press release "transmitted via telephone from Parris Island, S.C." According to an insider, "Dick might have been able to do a better job of 'managing the news,' but he was in the swamps of Parris Island the whole time, standing in a pay phone with a pocket full of dimes." Dick did not return to Washington, instead entering Yale Law School in a class with Hillary Rodham and Bill Clinton. Subsequently he was a clerk to Supreme Court Justice Harry Blackmun and was in the U.S. Attorney's Office in the District of Columbia when it was famously involved in the Abscam case. He then moved to Connecticut, where he served as attorney general for 20 years. In 2010, he was elected as a Democrat to the U.S. Senate from Connecticut.

CHRISTOPHER DeMUTH, 22, also went to Harvard. He was a student of political scientist Edward Banfield, rather than Moynihan. He knew Pat only slightly because he had been a busboy at Pat's Tuesday Joint Center luncheons, where his compensation was sitting in on the faculty discussions. From Cambridge, Chris went to Bedford-Stuyvesant, in Brooklyn, to work for civil rights leader James Farmer, who was being defeated by Shirley Chisholm in a newly formed congressional district. This led to a volunteer job at Nixon's transition headquarters in the Pierre Hotel and, through Len Garment, onto Pat's pick-up staff.

Pat first assigned Chris to figure out the pathology of the Model Cities program and from there to a task force, chaired by Banfield, which recommended combining Model Cities and other federal programs into the general-purpose revenue-sharing proposal that was a key part of Nixon's August 8, 1969, address on his domestic agenda. By the fall of 1969, Chris had moved into environmental policy, the area of most substantial innovation in Nixon's post-Moynihan period, including the creation of the Environmental Protection Agency and the passage of the Clean Air Act of 1970.

Chris entered the University of Chicago Law School in the fall of 1970, practiced law for several years, and in 1977 took a career turn into academics as a lecturer at Harvard's Kennedy School of Government and director of the Harvard Faculty Project on Regulation. His work on regulatory policy attracted the attention of newly elected President Reagan, who made him executive director of the White House Task Force on Regulatory Relief and administrator of the Office of Information and Regulatory Affairs in the Office of Management and Budget, jobs that were of immense importance in an administration that had made regulatory reform one of the pillars of economic revival.

When, in the mid-1980s, the American Enterprise Institute for Public Policy Research (AEI), a Washington think tank, was in the midst of serious financial and management difficulties, Chris was elected its new president. He led AEI for 22 years, reviving its finances, building its endowment to more than $100 million, attracting a staff of highly accomplished academics and intellectuals, and expanding its publications, conferences, and outreach operations. When Chris retired at the end of 2008, AEI was recognized as one of the nation's premier policy research centers, often described as a right-of-center analogue to the left-of-center Brookings Institution. Chris continues to study and write on issues of regulatory, fiscal, and legal policy as a distinguished fellow at the Hudson Institute.

CHESTER "CHECKER" FINN was closest to Pat; unlike the others, he had not yet left Harvard. At 25, Checker was Pat's graduate student at the School of Education, with an unconventional Ph.D. project that would grow out of observing how President Nixon developed his education policies. At the same time, he would work for Pat on everything that could be handed off to the young man who camped outside his office.

Checker continued his note-taking when transferred to the Ehrlichman staff in 1970. Ultimately, his book *Education and the Presidency* (Lexington Books, 1977) foreshadowed the future of a presidency "close-mouthed" and "staff busy." It is "an inward-looking policy process," he wrote. His working group on education "simply kept what it was doing to itself. Preoccupied with the need to resolve differences among its own members, the process of consensus building never moved beyond the executive branch. Congressmen and their aides were not consulted. Journalists were not briefed (until the day of the message) other than through a few intentional leaks. Education lobbyists were ignored."

After he left the White House to travel around the world, Checker became director of policy analysis at the University of Massachusetts and then special assistant for education to Governor Francis Sargent. When Pat went to India in 1973, Checker was with him as counsel to the ambassador. When Pat became a senator in 1977, Checker would become his legislative director. Between Moynihan assignments, Checker wrote books at Brookings. Post-Senate, he was appointed a professor at Vanderbilt and an adviser to Tennessee governor Lamar Alexander, another young man from the Nixon West Wing.

Rotating back in Washington in 1988, Checker was named assistant secretary of education. Along the way he kept writing books, including the much-acclaimed *The Educated Child* (coauthored with William Bennett and John Cribb) and the oft-cited *What Do Our 17-Year-Olds Know?* (coauthored with Diane Ravitch). He is now president of the Thomas B. Fordham Institute, with offices in Washington and Ohio, whose special focus is "the renewal and reform of primary/secondary education in the United States." Checker is also a senior fellow at the Hoover Institution.

JOHN PRICE, 30, was Pat's counsel, minder of the Urban Affairs Council, and point man on welfare reform. He went to Grinnell College in Iowa and to Oxford as a Rhodes Scholar. (He is a trustee of Grinnell and founding chairman of Americans for Oxford.) His Cambridge connections were Harvard Law and the Ripon Society, a new group of young liberal Republicans who operated out of a drab two-room office above the Harvard Square Theatre.

In 1968, John took leave of a job doing community development in Bedford-Stuyvesant to work for Nelson Rockefeller's failed campaign for the Republican presidential nomination. Should he then accept an offer from Nixon? He took this dilemma to his Bed-Stuy boss, John Doar. "You're a Republican aren't you? Why be squeamish about working for Richard Nixon? Just look at the other party." So he joined Len Garment, the campaign feeder into Pat's office. (John Doar's future would include running the House of Representatives staff that managed the Nixon impeachment.) After Pat's staff was dissolved, Ehrlichman gave John responsibility for overseeing the White House's health insurance/health care initiative. At the end of 1971, he returned to New York and began a 40-year career in finance, primarily at

Manufacturers Hanover Trust and its successor banks, where his positions included senior vice president for the mortgage banking and consumer finance subsidiaries, managing director in its investment bank, and head of government relations worldwide for Chase Manhattan.

In 2005, he was recruited as president and CEO of the Federal Home Loan Bank of Pittsburgh. He is now chairman of Mortgage Asset Exchange, an electronic platform for trading residential mortgages.

NOTES ON WRITING THIS BOOK

Eventually a writer with time, energy, and imagination will do the majestic multi-volume biography of Daniel Patrick Moynihan. In the meantime, Pat's history is being examined in significant segments. Indeed, to date two worthy contributions have been published by accomplished historians and skilled writers: James T. Patterson, *Freedom Is Not Enough: The Moynihan Report and America's Struggle over Black Family Life* (Basic Books, 2010), and Gil Troy, *Moynihan's Moment: America's Fight against Zionism as Racism* (Oxford University Press, 2013).

The Professor and the President attempts to follow this tradition, a difference being that the writer was there from the beginning. When I described to my friend Jim Grossman, the executive director of the American Historical Association, what I was struggling to do, he said I should think of the book not as a memoir or a history, but as a "dramatic narrative." And so it is.

And as Pat would write of his time in the White House, I too "make no pretense of 'disinterested objectivity.' I describe what I saw. My task at the time was to see things as clearly as I could manage; to delude myself as little as possible."

EVEN A FIRSTHAND observer needs to be reminded of certain details four decades after the fact. Many of those details are available in the *Public Papers of the Presidents, Richard Nixon, 1969, 1970* (U.S. Government Printing Office, 1971); at the Nixon Library, in Yorba Linda, California; and in the Moynihan Collection in the Manuscript Division of the Library of Congress. I too have some papers stored at the Library of Congress and some notes, regrettably few, that were written when I was in the White House.

While I have gone through all the Moynihan papers of these years, the very best are collected in Steven R. Weisman's *Daniel Patrick Moynihan: A Portrait in Letters of an American Visionary* (PublicAffairs, 2010). As for the history of the Family Assistance Plan, Moynihan got there first in *The Politics of a Guaranteed Income* (Random House, 1973); the other books of necessity being *RN: The Memoirs of Richard Nixon* (Grosset & Dunlap, 1978) and Henry Kissinger's *White House Years* (Little, Brown, 1979).

There is one remarkable "find" without which this book could not have been written in this form. Arthur Burns kept a diary, published as *Inside the Nixon Administration* (University Press of Kansas, 2010). As its editor, Robert H. Ferrell, explains, "The diarist wrote in two spiral notebooks, one marked thirty-nine cents, the other (larger) forty-nine," noting as well how difficult it was to decipher Burns's handwriting. The diary was not published in Burns's lifetime and clearly was not cleaned up for the ages. To Burns, Sargent Shriver was "more stupid than I had realized" and Federal Reserve chairman William McChesney Martin was a "pathetic slob!" He rated White House colleagues as "ineffective" or "indecisive." This is a diary that can be taken seriously.

There is a vast library of books by those who served on Nixon's White House staff, some ghostwritten, some written in self-defense. They are collectively fascinating in their attempts to try to figure out the "real" Nixon. In *With Nixon* (Viking Press, 1977), Raymond Price, his talented and dedicated speechwriter for 10 years, had to borrow Churchill's description of Russia: "a paradox wrapped in a contradiction inside an incongruity." William Safire, in *Before the Fall* (Doubleday, 1975), compared Nixon to a layer cake, his public face the icing.

For my immediate needs, however, there were only two volumes that I consistently returned to—*The Haldeman Diaries* (Putnam, 1994), the chief of staff's notes dictated late each night, and the aforementioned *Before the Fall,* full of documents and direct quotes by Safire, a careful writer with no axe to grind, who had made clear to Nixon that he would someday write a book. A third book, Leonard Garment's *Crazy Rhythm* (Times Books, 1997), was valuable to me in that he covered a number of specific moments shared with Moynihan. It is also very entertaining.

Journalists like to credit themselves with producing the first draft of history. But outside of wire service accounts of speeches and events, I was surprised at how little their reporting captured the churning dynamic within the Nixon White House when I was there. The struggle over welfare reform was hard to discern in the daily press, although this contentious debate hardly should have escaped notice. Partly this may reflect Nixon's hatred of journalists, which made his administration difficult to cover. While all presidents distrust the press, at least when in office, Nixon set the high-water mark. The most insightful reporting about the administration was John Osborne's column in the *New Republic,* "The Nixon Watch." (A volume of Osborne's columns from 1969 and 1970 was published by Liveright in 1971.)

In a sense, my book is twice-written: Everything that happened in 1969, when I was in the White House as Moynihan's deputy, is based either on what I saw or heard or on the first-hand accounts by others who were present. For 1970, when I was no longer in the West Wing, I have sometimes relied on secondary sources by others who were in a better position to judge an event, such as Godfrey Hodgson's *The Gentleman from New York: Daniel Patrick Moynihan* (Houghton Mifflin, 2000), which describes the attempt of radicals to trash the Moynihan home in Cambridge.

Still, I would learn that accounts appearing to be contemporaneous, written or spoken to describe a present moment, had to be held suspect if produced after the fact. The people of the 1969–70 White House would later be interviewed or write books. They had moved on and taken with them faulty memories or new agendas. Compare, if you wish, Don Rumsfeld's account of becoming OEO director in his 2011 book *Known and Unknown* (Sentinel) and the account in this book. Or differences when Moynihan, then a Democratic senator, looked back in a 1978 interview with A. James Reichley, author of *Conservatives in an Age of Change* (Brookings, 1981).

Yet one of the most useful attempts to understand what Nixon and Moynihan were trying to create came about on June 2, 2010, at a reunion of four people (Paul O'Neill, Robert Patricelli, John Price, and Jodie T. Allen) who had been importantly involved in putting together the Family Assistance Plan. Video of the Fifth Nixon Legacy Forum, cosponsored by the Nixon Presidential Library and the George Washington University School of Public Affairs, is available online at www.youtube.com/watch?v=IjWN-gy81wU.

A LOT OF people offered their time, talent, and goodwill to help turn this "dramatic narrative" into a book.

Checker Finn and John Price, two of the 1969 Moynihan Men, were always there when I needed to recharge my memory. I know this book would not be as accurate without them. Nor as much fun to write. Example of a little thing: My original draft placed Checker's desk outside Pat's door in the West Wing. But Checker reminded me that he actually shared a cubicle with Chris DeMuth in the EOB. What I apparently remembered, he said, was how he "camped out" at Pat's door, which is what this book now reports.

Another piece of research that might not turn up in more formal endnotes: Frank Raines, our summer intern in 1969, returned to Harvard to write a 130-page senior thesis on "The Genesis of the Family Assistance Program." Somehow he uncovered a copy for me; the key quote from Worth Bateman on how Johnson administration holdovers in HEW maneuvered to put the negative income tax on the Nixon administration agenda comes from Frank's interview with Bateman, on September 21, 1970.

Another marvelous piece of goodwill and good luck: James Rosen, once my student, in researching his book, *The Strong Man: John Mitchell and the Secrets of Watergate* (Doubleday, 2008), scrolled through the 100,000 pages on microfiche of Bob Haldeman's yellow pad notes—the basis for his nightly dictations into his famous diaries— and made his old professor a massive gift of extracts of whatever was said about Moynihan.

It was a joy too to have a steady stream of enthusiastic interns, whose assignments included photographing all the 1969 and 1970 papers in the Moynihan and Hess collections at the Library of Congress as well as adding up all the minutes that Moynihan, Burns, and Kissinger spent with Nixon. They are Avram Billig, Alicia Cho, Ariel Dobkin, Meredith Dost, Joseph Goodman, Aaron Locke, Kenneth Meyer, and Nik Royce. Their names will someday be as familiar as those of my past interns who are prominent journalists or went on to serve in a president's cabinet.

My colleagues at Brookings, my home now for over 40 years, keep finding ways to gently keep me in the twenty-first century. It is a talent not taught at school. And unique, I think, in large bureaucracies. My special thanks to Liz Valentini, Beth Stone, and Hillary Schaub in Governance Studies; to Laura Mooney and Sarah Chilton in the library; and to calm voices at the end of the help line in IT.

In writing the chapter about 1969, I am indebted to Rob Kirkpatrick's *1969: The Year Everything Changed* (Skyhorse, 2011); Roger Rosenblatt, *Coming Apart: A Memoir of the Harvard Wars of 1969* (Little, Brown, 1997); and Jules Witcover's *The Year the Dream Died: Revisiting 1968 in America* (Warner Books, 1997). Other books I liked for helping me see Nixon or Moynihan from different perspectives include Rowland Evans Jr. and Robert D. Novak's *Nixon in the White House: The Frustration of Power* (Random House, 1971); Tom Wicker, *One of Us: Nixon and the American Dream* (Random House, 1991); Robert A. Katzmann, ed., *Daniel Patrick Moynihan: The Intellectual in Public Life* (Johns Hopkins Universiy Press, 1998); and Richard Reeves's *President Nixon: Alone in the White House* (Simon & Schuster, 2001).

Among the friends who graciously answered questions about things I needed to know were Martha Derthick, Alvin Deutsch, William H. Frey, Len Garment, Arthur Klebanoff, Donald Lamm, Christopher Matthews, Richard P. Nathan, Paul H. O'Neill, and Geoffrey C. Shepard.

My most valued help came from four wise people who offered line-by-line reactions to my first draft: Frank Gannon, Luke A. Nichter, James P. Pfiffner, and Steven R. Weisman. Rarely has an author been blessed with such careful and caring readers.

And ultimately when it came time to turn all of the above into a book, there were the professionals of the Brookings Institution Press: Janet Walker, managing editor; Larry Converse, production manager; and Richard Walker, who always seemed to be a step ahead of what I wanted to do, which must be a definition of what a great editor does.

STEPHEN HESS
Senior Fellow, Emeritus
Brookings Institution
July 28, 2014

INDEX